THE RISE BACK

The Rise Back

Reclaiming Life After Suicide Loss, Pain, and Silence

Tiffaney Childers

Published by Game Changer Publishing

Paperback ISBN: 978-1-969372-26-1

Hardcover ISBN: 978-1-969372-27-8

Digital ISBN: 978-1-969372-28-5

GC GAME CHANGER
PUBLISHING
www.GameChangerPublishing.com

For those we have lost to the silence,
and for those who carry their stories forward.
You are the RISE BACK.

READ THIS FIRST

Thank you for buying my book and trusting me with your time and heart. I would love to stay in touch beyond this story.

Scan the QR Code Here:

THE RISE BACK

Reclaiming Life After Suicide Loss, Pain, and Silence

TIFFANEY CHILDERS

FOREWORD

When I first learned about Tiffaney Childers and the story behind *The Rise Back*, I didn't just see a survivor. I saw a woman who chose truth when silence felt safer, who chose connection when isolation felt easier, and who kept choosing her life when pain—both emotional and physical—kept pulling her toward giving up. That kind of courage is not loud. It's steady—the kind that transforms you from the inside out and, if you allow it, transforms the lives of the people you meet.

What you are about to read is not theory—it is lived truth. Tiffaney knows the ache of suicide loss, the shock, the unanswered "whys," and the way anniversaries approach like storms you can feel in your bones. She understands the quiet bargains we make with ourselves just to get through another day, and how easy it is to wear a smile while feeling shattered inside. If that is you, these pages will feel like someone has finally turned on the light and said, *"You are not broken. You are not alone. You matter."*

I believe community is a lifeline. When we share what is real, we create space for others to heal. Tiffaney doesn't perform strength—she lives it. She tells the truth about numbing pain without shame. She tells the truth about chronic pain that never takes a day off. She tells the truth about looking in the mirror and not recognizing yourself, and the day you decide to begin again. That's the turning point this book offers, with both compassion and courage.

Throughout these pages, she never pretends healing is quick or easy. She is not interested in rewriting the past—she is committed to honoring it while rebuilding a future. *The Rise Back* invites you to ask the questions that move you forward: Who can I lean on right now? What truth am I choosing today? What can I release so I stop exhausting myself in battles that can't be won? How can I endure this moment—one breath, one call, one page at a time? Where can I find rest so I can stand again tomorrow?

These questions will not erase grief, but they will give it shape. And they will give you a way through.

If you have felt alone because your loss is complicated... if you have hidden pain behind constant activity or a polished smile... if you have feared that healing means leaving love behind... this book will stay with you in the hardest moments and guide you toward something far stronger. It will lead you toward hope that can hold the weight of real life.

What I love most about Tiffaney's work is that she pairs raw honesty with practical tools. She gives you words for the days when you can't find your own. She shows you how to set boundaries that protect your peace, how to pause when your body feels like an alarm you can't shut off, and how to reach out for help before you close yourself off completely.

She also honors the truth that grief and gratitude can live in the same space. That's the difference between pretending you are fine and deciding you are worth the effort it takes to heal.

I see pieces of my own story in these pages—the slow climb back, the moments you fight for every bit of progress, and the choice to keep showing up when life feels heavier than you can carry. Our paths may be different, but I know the road she is writing about. That is why this book will speak to so many—whether you are grieving someone you love, living with chronic pain, rebuilding after identity loss, or simply tired of pretending you are fine. *The Rise Back* offers a way forward that is honest, compassionate, and entirely possible.

By the final page, you will believe healing is possible.

I am honored to introduce you to Tiffaney's book. May it meet you right where you are and help you take your next brave step.

Amberly Lago
USA Today Bestselling Author of *Joy Through the Journey* and *True Grit and Grace*, Top 1% Podcast Host, TEDx Speaker, Coach

CONTENTS

INTRODUCTION

This is not just a book about suicide loss. It's about loss in all its forms. This is a book about surviving the kinds of loss that leave you breathless, broken, and buried under the wreckage, just trying to survive.

This is about what happens after the funeral, after the silence, after the self-medicating.

After the pain will not let go.

My name is Tiffaney. I am a wife, a mother, a daughter. I was the person everyone could count on. I got things done. I had a good marriage and two amazing kids, and life felt steady and full. I saw my mom every day and talked to her at least three times a day. My dad lived nearby, and as I got older, our relationship grew closer and we saw each other all the time.

My relationship with my parents was similar to that of many adults. They helped me with the kids, offered advice, and showed up when I needed them.

My parents died by suicide—one year and five days apart.

What came next wasn't healing. It was chaos, rage, shame, silence, drinking, and darkness that I didn't know how to escape.

Then came the chronic pain.

A routine surgery triggered something I couldn't undo. I was diagnosed with CRPS—one of the most painful conditions a person can experience. It felt like my body had declared war on me. My nervous system was on fire. I couldn't move like I used to.

And maybe that's where you are, too.

The turning point that made me feel this book was necessary didn't come from a single event. It was more like a slow unraveling. One morning, after yet another night of unrelenting pain, I looked in the mirror and barely recognized myself. I was exhausted, not just physically but deep in my soul. I had lost my parents, my health, and my spark. I thought, *This can't be all there is.*

That moment was the beginning of everything this book represents: The Rise Back.

I didn't write this book because I have healed perfectly. I wrote it because I survived. This is not a polished self-help book. I am not a therapist or a doctor.

I am a woman who has walked through fire, and I'm still standing—barefoot, scarred, and rising.

I wrote this book to walk beside the ones who are silently crumbling. The ones who look like they have it all together. The ones pretending they are fine when, the truth is, they are just functioning to get through the day.

This book is *my* story and only mine. It is not a blueprint for all survivors, and it's not meant to represent anyone else's journey. It's just one woman's truth after losing both of her parents to suicide.

One thing I need to be clear on is this: I am not against medication, but I am for informed consent. I believe prescriptions can save lives, but I also believe you deserve full, honest information. What numbs your pain might also dull your power.

If medication helps you function, please take it, but also ask questions and do your research. Be awake.

Here is the truth I want to carve into your bones:

All life has meaning, no matter how it ends.

The way someone died will never erase who they were while they lived.

They were complex, loving, broken, beautiful people who mattered. And so do you.

Over the years, I have had the pleasure of working with the Local Outreach to Suicide Survivors (LOSS Team). LOSS Teams are made up of trained volunteers, many of whom are suicide loss survivors themselves. We partner with first responders and are dispatched to the scene of a suicide, often within minutes or hours of the death, to support the newly bereaved. We don't show up with scripts or solutions. We show up with lived experience, with presence, and with compassion.

Through my work with the LOSS team, I have had the honor of stepping into the darkest moments of others' lives to offer a hand, a hug, and a piece of understanding I wish I had had. This book is a continuation of that mission. It is my hand reaching out to you.

I want to offer courage to the lost, the lonely, and the broken after a suicide loss. I want to help you remember the strength that never truly left you. This doesn't mean erasing the pain. It means learning to coexist with it gracefully. There is a messy, undeniable power that comes from surviving what was meant to break you and choosing to rise anyway.

To the person outsourcing their worth to prescriptions and performance, this is for you.

To the ones who have stuffed their grief so deep that they can't find themselves anymore, this is for you.

To the brokenhearted, the barely hanging on, the soul-tired, this is for you.

You don't have to be fully healed to begin again. You just have to believe that pain doesn't get the final say.

Chapter One

NOT BEAUTIFUL, JUST BROKEN

I didn't wake up on Monday, July 2, 2007, expecting my life to fall apart. But that's the thing about suicide—it doesn't knock—it breaks down the door.

We had just returned from a family vacation in South Padre Island with my mom and stepdad. My son had been stung by a scorpion before we left, and by the time we got home, his big toe was swollen, red, and hot, and it was causing him excruciating pain. We took him to the doctor, who lanced it to try to drain the infection. Then we had to go back every day for the next few days to do the same thing. Each time, my son would scream in pain as they lanced the wound. He was just six years old, while my daughter had turned four the week before our trip to South Padre.

On our third visit to the doctor, they discovered that my son had developed an MRSA staph infection. They sent us to an orthopedic surgeon, who scheduled emergency surgery because the MRSA was so severe that it could enter his bloodstream. After the surgery, my son had to stay in the hospital for IV antibiotics through a port line.

We were in the hospital while my son recovered, and it was a beautiful summer morning—one that had no business being so gorgeous on the worst day of my life, when my stepdad called me. This was back when cell phones were not nearly as popular as they are now—people mostly used flip phones, and texting wasn't common. He said, "Your mom is dead."

"What do you mean, my mom is dead?" I asked. He explained that when he got to work, the caregiver we hired to take care of my mom called and said that my mom wasn't breathing and she looked dead. I hung up the phone and called my husband, who had just gotten into bed after working the night shift, and told him to come up to the hospital to stay with our son. "Mom is dead." That was all I could say. Just like that, my world split open. I had just talked to my mom the night before. She had called to check on my son.

I jumped into the car and picked up my sister, and we drove to our mom's house. When we arrived, the police and the funeral home were already there, and something in me short-circuited. I started laughing, and I couldn't stop. Not just a giggle, but uncontrolled laughter. My sister stared at me like I had lost my mind. Maybe I had just a little.

I went in to see my mom and made my sister go with me. She didn't want to, but I told her that she would regret it if she didn't. She still brings that up to this day because she had no desire to go inside. Mom was lying in bed, surrounded by pill bottles and handwritten notes that she had left me, my brother, and my sister. The police took those into evidence, and we wouldn't get them back for about six months.

Even as the funeral home attendants wheeled my mother's body out on a gurney, I was laughing so hard my stomach hurt. Horrified at my reaction but powerless to stop it, I kept saying between fits of laughter, "I'm sorry. I am so sorry." Looking back now, I am mortified by my response.

However, before you judge me, let me say this: I wasn't laughing because I thought the situation was funny. Not even a little. I was in utter shock. That kind of reaction is actually more common than people realize, and it's incredibly human. In the face of shock and trauma, our nervous system does what it can to survive the moment. It was my psyche's way of coping with the overwhelming reality of the situation.

I want everyone to understand that it doesn't matter what mistakes you made when you first learned of your suicide loss. Your response is valid, even if it was completely inappropriate. That's just your brain trying to protect you.

After they took her body away, my sister and I did what any rational, grieving daughters would do... we went to a Mexican restaurant and ordered the largest margaritas they served. Then another. And another. Tequila shots followed. We got spectacularly, inappropriately drunk in the middle of the afternoon, toasting a mother who would never share another meal with us. The burn of the tequila was the only thing that felt real in a world that had suddenly been turned upside down.

People always ask if there were signs. Lordy, there were billboards, but when you are living in the middle of a hurricane, you don't notice how hard the wind is blowing. You just try to stay upright.

To give some background, my mother was diagnosed with multiple sclerosis in her thirties. She had been in remission for about twenty-five years without any symptoms. However, in her late fifties, her MS returned with a vengeance, eventually leaving her in a wheelchair or scooter due to limited mobility. Throughout those years, she underwent numerous surgeries, including back and hip surgery, and the doctors armed her with an arsenal of pills: hydrocodone, OxyContin, Lyrica, Valium, and finally methadone patches, which are a synthetic opioid. She took all of those every day. Add in the alcohol, and my mother transformed into someone I barely recognized.

I was so naïve. At that time, I didn't know anything about addiction. I had no idea what it entailed. I was in my early thirties, and we didn't have the internet back then to research anything or understand the side effects of the pills. We trusted the doctors completely when they prescribed them. I didn't try to save her, not because I didn't love her, but because I didn't know she needed saving. The day of the phone call should not have shocked me, but it did. That's the hard truth about suicide: no matter how many warning signs you witness, the finality of it still hits like a wrecking ball.

My mom was hilarious, compassionate, and full of life. Vibrant, fun-loving, and deeply dedicated to both her job and her kids. That's why it was so painful to watch her slowly change before my eyes. To show just how serious her struggle with opioids became, I want to share a couple of stories.

One day, I was coaching my son's t-ball game, and I had dropped my daughter off at my mother's house for babysitting. After the game, when I went back to pick up my daughter, my mom said, "Don't forget the Coke I opened for her." So, I went over to the table to grab it, only to realize it wasn't a Coke at all. It was a Tecate beer. The two cans look similar because they are both red, and I guess my mother thought it was soda. Thankfully, my daughter had not drunk much of it, probably because she thought it tasted terrible.

There was another occasion during Halloween. We would always take the kids over to my mom's house to take pictures in their costumes. She had a bowl of candy corn by the front door, and when my son grabbed a handful, I noticed something white mixed in. I thought, *Wait. Let me see that.* Upon inspection, I discovered that my mother had spilled a bunch of pills into the candy corn. Fortunately, I caught it before my son consumed any of them.

I went to her house every few days to change the methadone patches on her back, and each time I pulled one off, it had eaten through her skin. She wasn't using them the way she was supposed to. One patch was meant to last seven days, but I would find two or three stuck on her at once, and they left open wounds where her skin should have been.

To give you an idea of how strong those patches were, I wouldn't even touch one with my bare hands, afraid that it would seep into my skin. Methadone is prescribed for chronic pain, but it is extremely potent and dangerous, especially when not closely monitored. It was originally developed in WWII as a long-acting pain reliever, and later, it became more widely used in addiction treatment for heroin addicts.

Many doctors in the early 2000s prescribed methadone off-label for pain, not always understanding how unpredictable and deadly it could be. In the late 1990s and early 2000s, not many people understood the full risks of opioids. Pharma companies, especially Purdue Pharma, aggressively pushed them (like OxyContin) as safe and non-addictive when used for pain. They were not regulated well during that time because the FDA trusted Purdue's manipulated data.

In 1999, the FDA approved methadone for chronic pain management despite its dangerously long half-life and complex effects on the brain. Doctors were handing out patches like Band-Aids and OxyContin like Halloween candy. They were not trained on how these drugs rewired the brain, especially when used long-term. Many believed that as long as a patient was in legitimate pain, addiction wouldn't be an issue.

Opioids don't just numb pain—they rewire the brain. They dull the body's alarms and twist the brain's reward system until the line between relief and survival blurs, and the brain stops thinking rationally. It whispered lies to my mom, convincing her that her life was a burden and that we would be better off without her. Opioids stole her clarity, her spark, and in the end, her life.

Nobody tells you how to grieve after a suicide. There were no support groups, no guides, no one saying, "Here is how you survive this." Back then, resources for suicide loss survivors were almost nonexistent. We didn't talk about mental health in school or college the way we do now. There was no Mental Health Awareness Day. No Suicide Prevention Day. No resources. No lifelines. Sure, Google existed, but smartphones weren't out yet. You couldn't just pull out a phone and search for resources. Even if you did find something online, it wasn't accessible the way it is today.

We didn't talk to my kids about it because I had no idea how to explain it. My husband and I never said the word "suicide" around them. My son was six, my daughter had just turned four, and we chose to move on without telling them how she died. I did the only thing I knew how to do—I shoved it down and kept going. I threw myself into motherhood and work, convincing myself that if I stayed busy enough, the sadness couldn't catch me.

That year, my husband and I felt the strain in our marriage. He tried, but as I often say, grief is a lonely country, with borders closed to visitors, and I wouldn't let him in. He avoided the subject, believing that discussing it would only upset me more. I kept looking to him for support, but he drifted further away because he didn't know how to help. I wanted him to take away my sadness, but he couldn't. Nobody could. His primary response was avoidance. We laugh about it now, but back then, I wrapped myself in a bubble, convinced it was the only way to keep from being hurt or abandoned.

My husband buried himself in work, and in response, I kept my bubble intact. I told myself, *Just stay silent and keep moving forward.* I couldn't just sit down and cry. I didn't have time. My kids were too little, and they needed a mom who was emotionally and physically present.

Together, my husband and I decided to ignore the word "suicide" and the reality that my mother had left us. We returned to our routines as best as we could. I packed school lunches, attended school events for my kids, and worked diligently, all while trying to be a mother who wasn't falling apart. I never allowed myself the luxury of breaking down because stopping meant feeling, and feeling meant drowning. I buried my feelings, my sadness, and my grief. Like a woman with no other choice, I kept pushing forward.

My son's toe eventually healed with a lot of physical therapy and antibiotics, but my emotional wounds were just beginning. If only they healed as quickly as physical ones. Instead, they festered beneath the surface, infecting everything they touched. The shame that comes with suicide crept in and began to affect every relationship I had. Friends stopped calling—or maybe I stopped answering—I honestly don't remember. The entire year after my mom's death is nothing but a thick fog.

My siblings and I went on with our lives, each coping in our own way. It was easier to pretend that everything was normal than to acknowledge the huge hole in our family. Out of sight, out of mind, but never truly gone. The loss of my mother had already left me with countless unanswered questions and a hollowness I carried around like a second heartbeat. Little did I know we were about to face another imminent loss. The fog that I was navigating would soon become even thicker, and the pain even more intense.

A SURVIVOR'S TRUTH:

Grief is messy. So is survival.
When someone you love dies by suicide, your brain will use whatever it can to keep you breathing—laughter, numbness, tequila shots, or a fog that erases months at a time.
They are simply life preservers that your psyche throws out when you are drowning.
None of it is wrong. It's survival.

THE RISE BACK TAKEAWAY:

You are not supposed to have all the answers in those first hours and days.
Everything is a blur of shock, disbelief, and raw emotion.
Don't beat yourself up for how you responded.
Whether you shut down, broke down, or did what you could to survive the moment, it was enough.

Be gentle with yourself.

Grief doesn't come with a manual, and there is no wrong way to react in the face of this kind of devastation.

Just keep breathing and know that your journey to healing will unfold in its own time.

TRANSFORMATION PROMPT:

What is one thing you wish someone had told you in the first days after your loss?

_____

_____

_____

_____

_____

The silence after a suicide loss shakes your soul, but your voice still matters. Speak. Scream. Write. Just don't stay silent.

Chapter Two

WHEN LIGHTNING STRIKES TWICE

*I*t was July 7, 2008, one year and five days after my mom took her life. It was a beautiful Texas summer evening, filled with the unmistakable sounds of locusts, crickets, and the rhythm of sprinkler systems. It felt like a normal evening, with nothing out of the ordinary, but I had already learned that tragedy doesn't always come with a warning sign.

Everything can seem fine—until it suddenly it's not. That day, my dad was watching my son because our regular babysitter had called in sick. He was happy to step in, so I dropped my son off before heading to work. My mom and dad had been divorced for quite some time, and both had remarried. My dad and I had become closer after I had kids. I am the baby of the family. My sister is eighteen months older, and my brother seven years older.

When I got off work, I picked up my son. He was seven then, and my daughter was five. He climbed into the car and was so excited, telling me about all the adventures he had with his papa all day. That evening, we had a birthday party for my son's best friend. His mom was one of my dearest friends, and the party was at a local minor league baseball game.

We loaded into the car, picked up my husband, and met my sister, along with a crowd of friends and family. Just as the first pitch was thrown, my phone buzzed. A text from a friend who lived down the street from my dad: *"Cop cars everywhere at your dad's house."*

I turned to my sister and said, "We need to go to Dad's."

We left my husband and kids at the baseball game, hopped in the car, and rushed toward my dad's house, knowing that the baseball field was about twenty minutes away. In the meantime, I called my best friend, who was also close with my dad, and asked him to run by my dad's house and check on him since he lived nearby.

During the twenty-minute car ride, I kept expecting to get a phone call from him, saying something like "Someone broke in" or "There was a fight down the street," but I never did. When we pulled up to his house, I saw my friend sitting on his motorcycle, and he wouldn't look at me. I couldn't help but think, *Why didn't he call me? Why is he not inside? Why won't he look at me?*

At that moment, my sister and I instinctively knew something was wrong. We got out of the car and noticed my stepmother sitting on the front porch in a chair, her head in her hands. We knew something bad had happened, but we just didn't know what.

We both fell to the ground right in front of the door, sobbing and crying. Even then, we still didn't know what was going on.

Apparently, my friend had gone to talk to my stepmom and got the rundown on what happened. He didn't know what to say to me and was pretty much unable to speak due to shock, so he didn't say anything at all. A police officer came outside and informed us that my dad had taken his life with a self-inflicted gunshot wound. My stepmother had been inside the house when it happened.

The shock was overwhelming and almost indescribable. I can't even explain that moment. There was just a stillness that didn't make sense. The atmosphere was solemn. I couldn't comprehend that this was happening again. What troubled me most was that there had been absolutely no signs. I kept asking myself, *What did I miss? I just saw him about an hour and a half ago. How could I not have seen this coming? What if I could have done something... anything... differently? Did he drop a hint that I didn't catch? What if I hadn't been so distracted when I picked up my son?*

We called my brother, who lived about six hours away. He was distraught, repeating, "Not again. I can't believe this is happening again." I have no idea whether I called my husband and told him, or what he did with the kids. I don't recall whether he kept them at the baseball game to shield them from the news or if my in-laws came to pick them up. To this day, I truly don't know. The thing about shock is that your brain goes foggy, and memories get fractured. Some details disappear, and they don't come back.

I immediately called a very dear friend of mine. She and her dad, who was like a second father to me, came over and sat with me for hours outside my dad's house, offering their love and silent support. They didn't have to say anything. Their presence mattered more than they even know to this day. My sister called her boyfriend, and we all sat outside together until they brought my dad's body out in a body bag on a gurney.

I will never forget the sound of locusts that night, a shrill, unrelenting chorus that wrapped itself around me. The air was thick and heavy with the kind of summer heat that sticks to your skin and makes it hard to breathe. As the sun went down, the crickets joined in, but the locusts were the loudest. They were high-pitched, piercing, and impossible to ignore. It felt like the whole night was closing in, sound pressing from every direction, heat clinging to my body, confusion tightening its grip. Even now, when I hear locusts, I am right back there on that night:

the sounds, the heat, the not knowing what had just shattered my world... *again.*

The police didn't tell us anything while they processed the scene. No one was allowed inside, so we never saw what was happening. They kept us out, and we just stood in the front yard in the thick summer night air. We paced the yard aimlessly, stunned and full of questions. I had so many *what-ifs*. So many *whys*.

It's different now, and I will explain why later. Today, police are more compassionate with survivors. Back then, they simply gave no information. Part of it was the process: a suicide can look like a homicide until the scene is fully examined. Was it a break-in? A neighbor with a gun? They had to rule everything out before calling it suicide.

I went home that night and cried and cried and cried. I felt so abandoned by both of my parents. It was the emptiest, hollowest feeling I have ever experienced in my life, and I hope I never have to feel that way again. Losing a parent is hard, but losing both by suicide breaks something inside you.

You walk differently. You love differently. You trust differently. You become a stranger in your own life, wondering, *Who am I supposed to be now? The two people who brought me into this world are no longer here.* It cracked something deep in my foundation, and I pushed it down so far I almost forgot it was there. I tucked it away, convincing myself I would deal with it later.

And now we were planning another funeral. The same friend who hosted the birthday party for her son the year before mentioned she knew someone at a carpet cleaning company. She said, "Let me call him. I think they can clean up the aftermath of the house after the gunshot wound." I remember thinking, *I didn't even know companies like that existed.* It had not crossed my mind that there would be blood and remnants left to deal with after a self-inflicted gunshot.

The next day, we went to my dad's house so the cleaning company could assess the damage. I stayed outside while my best friend went in with them. The mess must have been unbearable. I don't think I could have done it, so I will always be grateful that she stepped in. That's a good friend right there. You don't realize the mess death leaves behind—not only the emotional wreckage, but the physical aftermath too. As painful as it is, someone has to be paid to clean it up.

People sometimes ask if it was different losing my dad. Yes, it was very different. When Mom died, I had lived through so many hospital visits and potential overdoses that the emotional aspect of all that had already taken its toll.

In that state, my body reacted with laughter, not because anything was funny, but out of sheer exhaustion and shock. As for my dad, I was in complete and utter shock. At the time my dad left this world, I was still deeply grieving the loss of my mother.

In fact, I wasn't even grieving yet. At that point, we were still fighting to retrieve the suicide notes from evidence and were desperate to know what they said. I hadn't even started to process losing my mom, and I was so consumed by that battle that I hardly noticed what was happening with my dad. So when it came to my dad, his death was nothing but pure shock.

I spent the next eighteen years angry. Angry that they left. Angry at the mess. Angry that there was no goodbye. Angry that they missed my kids growing up. Angry that their final decisions completely changed the trajectory of my life.

Death is never easy, but most kinds of loss offer some kind of explanation. Illness gives you time to prepare. Old age allows you to say goodbye. A car crash or a heart attack, as sudden as they are, can still be understood. Even an overdose or an accident, as tragic as they feel, can eventually be pieced together. Those deaths offer a thread of closure, a way to make sense of what happened. Suicide offers none of that.

Suicide makes no sense. The brain is not designed to comprehend it. I don't think our brains are equipped to process the idea of someone taking their own life. The kind of grief that comes with suicide loss is confusion, rage, guilt, shame, and silence. If a person dies from a heart attack, we don't question their eating habits, drinking, or smoking. We simply accept it.

Suicide is much harder to accept due to the stigma, assumptions, and judgment that weigh down an already unbearable loss. You learn pretty quickly that no one wants to speak openly about suicide. People avoid the word because it makes them uncomfortable. Well, it makes me uncomfortable too—if that helps any. So, I shut down, stayed busy, and survived. But surviving is not the same as healing. Surviving is a cage. Healing is the key.

A SURVIVOR'S TRUTH:

You are not broken beyond repair.

I don't care how many times you have been hit by grief, trauma, or loss. Your soul is still in there, buried under the rubble, waiting to rise. Sometimes, your brain does you a favor and blacks out some of the details.

You didn't miss the signs.

You didn't fail them. Suicide is not something you could have controlled or cured with more love or more effort. That blame? That shame? It doesn't belong to you. This pain is proof that you cared deeply. That you still do. But you were never meant to carry any of it. Their silence is not your shame to carry.

THE RISE BACK TAKEAWAY:

Breathe. Literally.

Put your hand on your chest and feel it rise. That's your body fighting for you. You don't need to solve anything right now. You just need to breathe through this minute and then the next.

You didn't cause this.

You could not have prevented this. You are allowed to grieve without guilt. Tape it to your mirror. Screenshot it. Burn it into your brain if you have to. You are not responsible for someone else's choice to leave.

TRANSFORMATION PROMPT:

What pain have you been carrying for so long that it has become part of your identity?

_____

_____

_____

_____

_____

They will always be part

of your story, and you get

to write the rest. Write it bold.

Write it beautiful. Live it

in a way that honors every

breath they couldn't catch.

Chapter Three

WE DON'T TALK ABOUT THAT

fter my dad's death, we held a packed funeral. He was an avid hunter and had lots of friends from all walks of life. My stepmother planned the entire service, including the choice of church and pastor, which left us with little involvement in the details.

As I sat in the front row, the pastor began to speak about whether my dad was in Heaven or Hell. His words shocked everyone in attendance. This was a room full of broken hearts, and the man we trusted to bring us comfort and peace, instead, planted seeds of doubt and shame. That's what suicide often leaves survivors with: doubt and shame.

Many of my dad's friends were visibly upset and began walking out. I kept looking back as more and more people left in disgust over what the pastor had said. That moment shattered relationships. It was just another wound layered on top of a loss, another silence I didn't know how to fill.

Here's the truth: all life has meaning, no matter how it ends. The way someone died will never erase who they were while they lived. Their worth didn't vanish with their last breath, and their story doesn't become less sacred because of how it ended.

We stopped speaking to my stepmother after that day, and we never really spoke to her again. Grief often drives us to look for someone to blame, and she became our focus. Instead of supporting one another, we turned against each other and blamed her for being present when it happened. I don't know if they argued or what really happened in those final moments. Ultimately, it doesn't matter now.

Two weeks after the funeral, my husband took a new job that required him to go out of state for training for the next year. He came home only twice during that time. I tried to be proud of him. I tried to hold everything together, but inside, I was unraveling. I felt so abandoned by yet another person in my life: first my mom, then my dad, and now my husband. While he was trying to build his career, which I am extremely grateful for, there I was, drowning in grief and feeling so alone. Life doesn't pause for grief —the bills don't stop coming, work still demands your attention, and the laundry keeps stacking up. Life moves on whether you are ready or not.

So, there he went, leaving me with two small children while I was overwhelmed with grief. I was surrounded by lots of people during that time, yet I felt like the loneliest person on the planet. After this funeral, even more friendships faded. It's strange how suicide creates such silence. People don't ask questions, and they don't bring the suicide up. You get one awkward "I am so sorry," and then everyone pretends as if it never happened, like my life didn't just implode.

Nobody hands you a manual for surviving this kind of loss. I had no clue what to do. I was raising two kids with a heart full of pain, so I did what came naturally: I stuffed it down, drank it down, and kept moving like nothing was broken.

I also learned quickly that talking about it made people uncomfortable. So I made myself small, carried the weight quietly, and smiled in public. The truth is, when you are grieving a suicide loss, you don't want solutions—you want safety. Sometimes that just means having someone who can sit in the silence with you. Unfortunately, not many people can.

I have always said that strangers become friends and friends become strangers after a suicide loss—and almost every survivor nods in agreement. Suicide shakes people's sense of control and safety, so they avoid it. They don't know what to say, so they say nothing.

I think grievers become too much for some people, not intentionally, but because the pain from suicide loss is too raw, too unfixable, and too outside the realm of socially acceptable grief. People are okay with sadness but not with suffering. Most people want to be helpful, but they struggle to sit with pain that can't be solved.

Eventually, I grew territorial with my heart, convinced the world wasn't safe. After a loss like this, every relationship feels like a risk. You brace for abandonment before it even happens. Over time, I built a circle of people who could sit with the uncomfortable. Still, the fear of being left never fully left me. It became muscle memory, reinforced by the reality that most people slowly disappeared—except for a few good friends and my family. I am grateful to the ones who stayed and loved me through this chaos.

After both deaths, I still didn't tell my kids much. I thought I was protecting them, but in truth, I didn't know what to say. I think children are often the forgotten grievers in a family. They experience the same emotions we do, so I want to remind people to share their thoughts and tears with them and make them feel loved and included. They may not have the words, but they feel everything. After my mom and dad died, we didn't talk to the kids about it. We never said, "They died by suicide." They were too young to even understand that word. They just knew that Papa had died and that we had gone to another funeral, same as with Mamaw.

It's crucial to talk to kids about these things, but I said nothing to mine. This wasn't because I didn't care, but because I didn't know what to say. Nobody tells you how to explain something this complex to a child. In the days, months, and even years after losing my parents, I found myself paralyzed when it came to talking to my children about what happened. I was terrified of planting a seed I couldn't take back. I didn't want them to think suicide was an option, a solution, or something that ran in our blood. I was afraid that if I said that word out loud, I might somehow make it seem acceptable. So, I just stayed silent.

However, here is what I have learned: silence doesn't protect our children—it isolates them. They can feel the heaviness even if they don't have the words for it yet. When we don't give them the truth, they fill in the blanks with something even scarier. That silence becomes its own kind of story, one that is harder to rewrite.

I wasn't wrong in wanting to protect them. Every parent wants to shield their child from pain, but avoiding the conversation doesn't erase the reality. What helps is how we talk about it: with care and honesty that is grounded in love. We need to remind our children that no matter how heavy life feels, there is always another way.

Everything can be figured out.

That's what I want my kids to know... that even when life is messy, dark, and overwhelming, there is help. There is hope. There are tools and people to talk to. There is a future worth fighting for, even if it doesn't feel like it in the moment.

Talking about suicide doesn't plant the idea. *Not* talking about it can.

I don't want to give my children a legacy of silence. I want them to know that pain is survivable and that life is always worth staying for. That's exactly why I wrote this book.

Honesty doesn't have to be graphic, and protecting innocence doesn't mean avoiding the truth. Silence leaves room for fear, and talking with kids can give them a sense of security even in the middle of loss.

Here is what I wish I knew back then—a way to talk to children about suicide that is real, safe, and rooted in love.

If They are Little (Ages 0–5)

They don't understand death fully, only that someone is gone and life feels different. Keep it short, safe, and reassuring.

"Grandpa died. His body stopped working, and he can't come back."

Avoid phrases like "went to sleep," which can cause fear around bedtime. Let them ask questions, and keep reminding them: "You are safe. You are loved. This wasn't your fault."

At some point, those little ones grow into children who ask more questions and want to understand the "why." That's when the conversation shifts.

If They are Growing (Ages 6–9)

They will want to know "why," but don't need every detail.

"Grandpa died because something in his brain stopped working the right way."

Avoid clinical terms that can confuse them. Answer only the question they asked, and reassure them: "He loved you very much. You didn't do anything wrong."

As they move into the preteen years, the need for truth deepens, but so does their sensitivity to tone, secrecy, and shame.

If They are Preteens (Ages 10–13)

They can handle more truth, but how you say it matters.

If they ask directly whether it was suicide, be honest but gentle:

"Grandpa died by suicide. That means he ended his own life, but it wasn't because he didn't love us, his brain was very sick and he couldn't see another way."

If they don't ask, you can still explain without using the "word" right away:

"Grandpa died because his brain got so sick that it made him believe there was no other option."

Acknowledge the confusion and mixed emotions. Let them know it's okay to feel angry, sad, or numb, sometimes all at once.

By the time they are teenagers, they don't just want the truth —they want to be trusted with it.

If They are Teens (Ages 14+)

They want honesty, facts, and respect.

"Grandpa died by suicide. We don't fully understand why."

Share your own emotions openly. Offer options for support, but don't push. Remind them: "You don't have to pretend to be okay. This doesn't define you."

Truth for the Parent (or Grandparent, or Caregiver)

There is no perfect script. You will not have all the answers, and you don't need to. What matters most is that your child knows they are safe, loved, and never to blame.

Remind them again and again:

"What happened wasn't your fault. You are safe. And you are not alone."

There is another layer to all this that no one talks about. It's not just the grief, and it's not just the silence. It's the *shame*. Shame that they died that way. Shame that makes you feel like you owe an explanation for someone else's death. Shame that lives in the silence after someone says, "I am so sorry for your loss," and then tilts their head, waiting for you to explain how, like suicide needs a backstory to be valid. Shame that creeps in every time someone says, "But they seemed so happy," like you are the one who missed the signs, and that is why they are gone. The sideways glances. The awkward silences. The feeling that you have to explain their death, soften it, or lie about it altogether. Nobody talks about the shame, which can feel heavier than grief.

When the funeral is over and you return to your life, that's not where grief ends. It's often where another layer begins. Secondary losses are the invisible ripples no one warns you about. You lose friends who don't know how to be around you anymore. You lose your sense of safety, the belief that tomorrow is guaranteed, and the version of yourself who trusted that the world is fair.

For some, it's the loss of financial stability, the job they could no longer focus on, the marriage that couldn't withstand the weight, or the faith that once anchored them. Others lose their joy, their motivation, their ability to dream without fear. These changes don't crash in all at once. They creep in quietly, piece by piece, until one day you realize entire parts of your life have slipped away, and not just because of the death, but because of everything the death took with it.

If you have ever felt this way, you are not broken. You are living through the aftershocks of loss. This is what happens when death takes more than a person—it takes a piece of the life you thought you knew.

You might feel like you failed your loved one, questioning every memory and conversation. You replay each moment over and over in your mind, wondering if people are judging or blaming you. You think, *Maybe if I had said just one thing differently, noticed something sooner, or shown up just thirty minutes earlier...* You question everything, as if stuck on a broken record.

I didn't say this out loud for a long time, but I am saying it now: **Liar, liar, brain on fire. These are all lies that grief tells us after a suicide loss.**

Grief doesn't just make you cry. It talks out loud, and most of the time... *it lies.*

Especially after a suicide loss.

There is a cruel voice that shows up, the one that sounds like your own, but it's not truth speaking. It's trauma and shock. It's guilt doing what guilt does best: rewriting the story and blaming you for what happened.

Here are some of the dirtiest lies my brain whispered in the silence:

- **You should have seen it coming.**

As if love is some kind of crystal ball. As if we are supposed to have some sixth sense that overrides everything someone tries to hide.

- **You were not enough to keep them here.**

This one hurts. It plants the idea that your love wasn't strong enough to keep them here when, actually, their pain was just louder in that moment.

- **If you had answered that last call... maybe...**

This is the grief loop. You replay, regret, and rewrite. None of it brings them back, and none of it is fair.

- **You don't get to grieve this out loud.**

Suicide makes people uncomfortable. No one wants to ask what really happened, and if they do, you feel judged or blamed.

- **You should be over this by now.**

Healing takes time, and grief doesn't have an expiration date.

All of these are lies. Cruel, exhausting lies. They are so convincing that they can keep you silent. They can keep you sick. They can bury your voice, your story, and your healing if you let them.

I want my readers to know that if you have experienced a loss to suicide, you didn't cause it. You couldn't have stopped it, and you don't have to carry the burden of shame.

I said this earlier, and I will say it again. If someone dies of a heart attack, we don't blame them. We don't say, "Well, they shouldn't have eaten all that fast food," "Maybe if they had worked out more, " or "That's what happens when you smoke for twenty years." We don't dissect their choices at the funeral—we grieve them, remember the good, tell stories, and offer comfort.

But when someone dies by suicide, suddenly, it becomes a question of blame: "What were they thinking?" "Why did they not ask for help?" "How could they do this to their family?" We weaponize their pain and make their death their fault, or worse, a family member's fault. Mental pain is not a moral failure. Suicidal despair is not a character defect. It's a medical, emotional, and spiritual crisis that deserves compassion, not criticism. We need to stop downplaying the impact of invisible wounds, treating them as less real than visible ones. A heart attack may stop a heartbeat, but so can hopelessness, and both deserve our grace.

A lot of people refer to depression as a mental illness, and maybe that's true in some cases. I have always wrestled with the word "illness." The whole concept of mental health and mental illness still feels so murky to me. What I do know is that suicide is not always about a diagnosis, and not everyone who struggles has a label attached. A good friend of mine says it best: "Not everyone with a mental health diagnosis dies by suicide, and not everyone who dies by suicide has a mental health diagnosis."

Suicide is never just one thing. It's not always depression... or trauma... or addiction. Sometimes, it's just the perfect storm. Maybe it's caused by the brain misfiring, hormones crashing, pain that won't stop, silence that suffocates, or pressure that becomes too much. Sometimes it's even the very medication meant to help that backfires, twisting relief into something unbearable. That storm doesn't always come with warning signs, and it doesn't always come with a clear reason.

Suicide is not black and white. It's human, and it's messy. We don't talk about being mad at the person we miss the most. I was angry for so many years. I was mad at my mom for leaving, mad at my dad for following, mad that they didn't fight harder, and mad that my siblings and I were left to carry it all. Then I was ashamed for even feeling that way.

Anger is a part of grief, too. It's messy and uncomfortable, and if we don't name it, it owns us. We don't talk about how love and fury can live in the same breath, and maybe it's time we start. Maybe we need to stop shaming the parts of grief that don't fit the Hallmark sympathy card. Maybe we can start saying out loud, "I miss them, and I am mad... and I am still trying to make peace with both." Healing doesn't ask us to choose between love and pain. It invites us to hold both... and still keep going.

Here is what I learned the hard way: staying silent doesn't heal anything. Silence keeps the pain circulating, and it doesn't go away. It just finds new ways to leak out, through anger, exhaustion, illness, or disconnection. Silence became a second wound, and the longer I held it in, the heavier it got.

Grief doesn't just live in your head and heart. It lives in your body, in your breath, in the way you tense up when a certain date creeps closer. The anniversary of their death. Their birthday. The holidays they loved. Even if you try to ignore the calendar, your body seems to know. You feel it in your chest before you even realize why you are short-tempered, restless, or on the verge of tears. These days are circled in invisible ink, and no matter how much time passes, they have a way of finding you.

Once I started speaking the truth, even the messy, uncomfortable, not-so-pretty parts, I could finally feel myself beginning to come up for air. It gave me space to feel and keep moving forward. It is not just about what we don't talk about. It's about what we *have* to start talking about so we can finally begin to breathe again.

A SURVIVOR'S TRUTH:

If you found yourself reaching for a bottle, retreating from the world, or losing your voice in the aftermath, it doesn't mean you are weak.
It means you were trying to survive something unthinkable.
It means you needed relief, and you took the path that was right in front of you.

And if it's been months or years, and you still have not asked for help?

You are not behind.

You are not broken.

You are exactly where so many of us have been: silent, hurting, and trying to keep it all together.

You don't owe anyone a polished version of your grief.

You are not too much.

You are not alone.

And you don't have to whisper.

THE RISE BACK TAKEAWAY:

Say one thing out loud that you have been holding in.

Just one. Write it, speak it, scream it into a pillow—I don't care how it comes out, but let it come out.

Grief is not meant to be swallowed.

Start small. Start honest.

And when the silence tries to creep back in?

Talk anyway. You don't owe the world silence. You owe yourself freedom.

TRANSFORMATION PROMPT:

What weight are you carrying that you no longer want to hold?

_____

_____

_____

_____

_____

You can't heal what you refuse to speak.
Silence may protect others, but it poisons you.

Chapter Four

BURIED BENEATH THE NOISE

This is the part that I call "the messy middle," and it lasted more than a decade—a long stretch when I wasn't falling apart, but I wasn't healing either. I was surviving, numbing, performing, doing everything I could to outrun the silence inside me.

My husband worked long hours and was away every other week for work, so I threw myself into motherhood. I also started CrossFit and stuck with it for eleven years. I became obsessed with CrossFit because I needed to feel strong, and I didn't know how to feel broken. In CrossFit, I could beat my previous performance. I could time it, control it, push through it, which is so unlike grief.

At forty, I was in the best shape of my life, physically. I survived each day knowing that if I stopped moving, I might never get back up. I became a master of over-functioning. If there was a task to do, a meeting or school event to attend, a party to plan, I was three steps ahead. I worked hard every day, crushed it at the gym, showed up for work, smiled, and small-talked my way through the day.

Productivity became my drug, and chaos my comfort zone. As long as I was moving, I didn't have to feel. I spent all my energy trying to look okay. I thought that if I looked good and my body was strong, then maybe no one would notice that I was crumbling underneath. I wasn't thriving. I was surviving on adrenaline and more alcohol than I care to admit. I was terrified that if I slowed down, everything would catch up to me.

Movement was my medication, and CrossFit was my addiction. Speaking of medication, I tried every antidepressant on the market. Every time I said, "I just feel sad," I left with another prescription. I was chasing peace and happiness through a pill bottle. Some medications dulled the sorrow, but no one warned me that they would dull everything else, too, like my joy, my motivation, my spark. I didn't feel alive—I felt sedated.

I have since learned that antidepressants can actually make things worse before they get better. For some people, especially in the first few weeks, certain medications may increase suicidal thoughts, emotional blunting (which means feeling emotionally dull and no longer finding things as pleasurable as you used to), or severe restlessness. The FDA eventually issued a black box warning for many antidepressants because of the risk of increased suicidal ideation, especially in adults under twenty-five.

Of course, I was never told that by my doctor. I was in my early thirties and still got lost in that fog. When one pill didn't work, I was told to give it about six weeks, to try another, or to take something else along with it. I was on a cocktail of SSRIs, SNRIs, and anti-anxiety meds. Each one promised relief, yet they all left me feeling more detached and flat.

I know this might ruffle some feathers, and let me be clear... I am not anti-medication. I am pro-informed consent. There is a difference. I am not here to tell you what to take or not to take. I am here to tell you to *ask the questions*. Demand full transparency. Advocate for informed consent, not blind trust. SSRIs can increase suicidal thoughts. Suicide risk rises in the first two weeks of starting antidepressants. A sudden shift in mood for the better might mean the decision has been made.

Grief is not a mental illness. It is love that has lost its landing place. But somewhere along the way, we started treating grief like a diagnosis. We gave it codes, created checklists, and handed people forms that were never designed with grief in mind. Take the PHQ-9, for example. It's a nine-question form you have probably filled out in a doctor's office or waiting room. It asks things like, *"How often have you felt little interest or pleasure in doing things?"* or *"Have you had thoughts that you would be better off dead?"* On paper, it looks like a neutral screening tool for depression. But here is the truth most people don't know: the PHQ-9 wasn't born out of pure science. Pfizer bankrolled it in the 1990s as part of a marketing strategy to roll out antidepressants, especially Zoloft. It became the easiest way to identify "patients" who might need medication, and while it's still widely used today, it was never designed to capture the complexity of grief. Grief is not a chemical imbalance, and it's not something you can score on a form. It's a story. A crack in your life. A love too heavy and too real to be tucked away.

And here is where we have gotten it wrong: when we funnel grief into the same pipeline as depression, we end up prescribing pills where we should be offering presence. That doesn't mean medication has no place. It can be lifesaving for some, but more often than not, grief needs something different. It needs grief therapy, not generic "mental health" therapy that tries to make the pain disappear. Grief therapy says: Let's honor what you lost. Let's make room for the tears, the rage, the silence, the questions. It doesn't rush you. It doesn't label you broken. It walks beside you until your grief finds its rightful shape in your life.

At that time, what I needed wasn't just a prescription—I needed a real conversation. You can't numb the sadness without numbing the light. Those pills muted my spirit and sedated me into silence. Finally, after trying so many antidepressants, I agreed to take trazodone. I had no idea what it was, but the doctor said it was an anti-anxiety drug combined with a sleep aid. It definitely helped me sleep, which was something I had not done in two years, as the silence at night was so loud and the weight of grief and abandonment so heavy that rest was impossible.

I took one little pill of 150 milligrams every night for eighteen years. I stayed on trazodone through grief, parenting, pain, surgeries, and survival. It became part of my nightly routine, like brushing my teeth and saying my prayers. Eventually, the fog it caused felt normal. Eighteen years later, I am weaning off of trazodone, and it has been pure hell. I have had brain zaps, dizziness, and raw emotions crawling out of my skin—and, oh my gosh, the insomnia.

This is not a story from the mountaintops. This is me, mid-climb. I am finally choosing clarity over sedation, and I am finally choosing to feel everything I have spent years running from.

In the chaos of the messy middle, I tried counseling... once. It was a disaster. The therapist had zero experience with suicide loss or trauma. I left feeling frustrated, dismissed, unseen, and angry. That experience taught me that not all therapists are equipped for this kind of grief. You can't talk someone through suicide loss with surface-level coping skills. I didn't go back, and honestly, that one bad session kept me from seeking help again for a long time. If you have been there, I see you.

Also during this time, I tried attending a local church's survivors group. On my first visit, one woman spoke about how people don't look the same when they go to heaven, claiming we will never know what our loved ones look like in the afterlife. I sat there, stunned. I never went back after that night.

In 2011, death knocked again. My father-in-law had just come home from dialysis. My husband picked him up, with our two young kids in the backseat, and brought him to our house to relax for a little while until another family member could get him and take him home. Minutes later, he collapsed on our kitchen floor. My husband dropped to his knees and started CPR, while our ten-year-old son stood nearby, on the phone with 911, relaying instructions. Our eight-year-old daughter watched, frozen.

I had just gotten off work, and as I rounded the corner to our house and saw the ambulance, fire truck, and police cars outside our home, my heart dropped. I thought, *Oh, my gosh! What has happened?* They put my father-in-law in the ambulance, and he later passed away at the hospital.

Just like that, we were grieving all over again. I had no idea how to comfort my husband or help my kids process what they had just witnessed. We buried another loved one, and I buried pieces of myself with him.

After my father-in-law passed, we did what so many families do and went right back to work. There were bills to pay, kids to raise, and no space to fall apart. Remember the old saying, "Time heals all wounds"? That's a lie. Time doesn't heal anything... *You* do.

Healing is not automatic. It requires intention and happens one brutal, brave breath at a time. Time gives you space to rebuild around the scars, but it definitely doesn't heal all wounds. Time might give you distance, but it doesn't do the work for you. It might soften the edges, but it doesn't erase the scars.

Men often compartmentalize far better than women. My husband boxed up the pain, put it on a shelf, and went back to work. That's how he stayed functional. Meanwhile, I carried it all... my grief, his grief, our kids' grief. It leaked into everything in me.

Grief doesn't disappear. It just settles into your body and grows stronger in the dark. All the running, numbing, and over-functioning only gave my trauma a deeper place to root. I was keeping it together, raising kids, showing up, smiling, and surviving. I cheered for my kids at every game, every match, every gymnastics meet, every milestone. As I watched them turn into incredible human beings, I saw their strength and thought, *Maybe I didn't mess up parenthood after all.*

My husband was still out of town every other week for work, sometimes even longer, and he did a great job providing for our family. Grief was still there, heavy and constant, but we didn't dare talk about it. We stayed busy because it was easier than stopping. School drop-offs, work, tennis, gymnastics, grocery runs—life kept moving, and we kept up the pace. We looked like we were doing fine, but really, we were just avoiding the pain. We didn't talk about death, or really anything that hurt, for that matter. There was no room for that and definitely no room to fall apart.

I kept my circle small and safe for so many years. My brother, my sister, and I formed a triangle of survival. We didn't have all the answers, but we had each other, and that was enough. We were the only ones alive who had walked through the same hell, and we spoke a language only the three of us knew.

However, we were all drowning in our own ways. We held each other up, but sometimes, we also enabled each other's worst impulses. Being the baby of the family, I was by far the loudest and wildest of the three of us—and, hands down, I was the best binge drinker. If chaos needed a captain, I was it. I poured the shots, lined them up, and dared you to keep up. My motto was "YOLO! You Only Live Once!" This sounds like total freedom, but really, it's just a prettier name for self-destruction. Grief can make you wild—it's not always expressed as crying in bed. My grief erupted as dancing on tables and chasing chaos.

My stepdad eventually got remarried to a kind, wonderful woman. He didn't have to stay in our lives, but he did, and that meant more than I probably ever told him.

I want you to know that the messy middle wasn't all bad. In fact, there was far more joy than sadness. I take deep pride in the way I raised my kids during that time. They grew up kind, good, and resilient. Somehow, I managed to keep their world steady while carrying a grief I never fully processed. That's a kind of strength we don't talk about enough: raising kids while carrying grief, no matter what type of loss you have lived through.

My husband and I, despite the unspoken heaviness, didn't break. Some days, surviving was our only love language. Through the years, I developed several unhealthy coping mechanisms. Drinking, staying in constant motion, and building emotional walls that affected everything around me. What I didn't under-stand back then was how common this really is after a suicide loss. When your world is shattered, survival often looks like distraction, denial, or numbing. These coping mechanisms may not be healthy, but they are human. It is the nervous system's way of protecting you when the pain feels unbearable.

Many survivors find themselves doing whatever it takes to keep moving, to avoid the silence, or to build barriers strong enough to keep the hurt at bay. It doesn't mean you are broken. It means you are grieving the unthinkable in the only way you know how. It took me years to realize that avoiding my feelings wasn't helping me heal. It was merely postponing the inevitable reckoning. The grief was still lingering inside. That's the crazy thing about it. It just waits until you are ready to fall apart.

The messy middle is where grief and gratitude coexist, where you are still building something beautiful amidst the pain. I believe that's the essence of it all: it's okay to feel both joy and sorrow. You can grieve *and* grow. You can carry the weight of unanswered questions and still feel incredibly grateful for the life you are building.

For many survivors, happiness feels complicated. Guilt is often tied to moments of joy, almost as if you are betraying the person you lost if you smile too much or move forward. If that's you, I want you to know this... you don't have to earn your joy. You are allowed to feel the light again. You are allowed to laugh, love, and find beauty in your days.

Joy doesn't mean you have forgotten. It doesn't mean the pain is gone. It simply means you are choosing life, and that is not betrayal—that's resilience. You are allowed to hold sorrow in one hand and gratitude in the other. We should not feel guilty for embracing joy and the positive experiences in our lives. I avoided my grief for so long that I probably overcompensated with joy and happiness to avoid facing difficult emotions and distract myself from the sadness.

One of the things I carry that bothers me to this day is that my parents never got to watch my kids grow up. They missed birthdays, school plays, and first dances. They missed the kind, beautiful humans that my children have become. I am only speaking from the perspective of losing my parents to suicide, but no matter the loss you have experienced, whether it's a parent, child, spouse, or friend, the pain is real. The ache for what could have been and the milestones missed, or for the love that never got to finish unfolding... It's all devastating.

I convinced myself that I was completely healed by the end of the messy middle, and I truly believed it. In reality, I didn't spend any time actually healing. I never did the work. I just tricked myself into thinking I was okay. I thought that if I ignored my feelings long enough, they would disappear. If I could drink just enough to numb the pain, then I wouldn't have to feel the weight of everything. But the pain was always waiting for me in the morning.

I didn't know what grace was back then—I was very hard on myself. I never gave myself grace, not once. When someone tried to extend grace to me, I couldn't accept it because I didn't know how. I was too used to performing, perfecting, and pushing through. Rest felt lazy, and compassion felt weak. The idea of receiving kindness, especially from myself, felt uncomfortable. I thought that if I softened, I would fall apart. The truth is, I was already falling apart, just silently. I measured my worth by how much I could carry without breaking.

I call this high-functioning grief. After trauma, we learn to measure our worth by how well we hold it together. No one asks if you are really okay, but everyone praises your strength, composure, and ability to keep going like nothing happened, for pushing through, for being so strong. So, strength becomes your identity, but in reality, it's not strength—it's survival. I started confusing endurance with worth, thinking, *If I just don't fall apart, I am doing something noble.* What I was really doing was disappearing and shrinking myself down to a role I didn't choose: the one who never falls apart. Breaking felt like failure to me, like weakness, like letting people down.

Now I realize that the more I carried without breaking, the more disconnected I became from my body, my truth, and myself. Eventually, that weight catches up with you. It shows up in your health, your relationships, and in the silence you keep. You can think you are holding it together, but it always leaks out somewhere.

Somewhere along the way, society taught me to wear exhaustion like a badge and to hide my pain so no one gets uncomfortable. Society believes that as women, we are expected to nurture, lead, and endure, all without asking for help. Where did that even come from? Because, again, that's not strength—that's survival, and we all deserve more than just surviving.

A SURVIVOR'S TRUTH:

You can be the strongest one in the room and still be falling apart inside.
Survival is not the same as healing, and pretending you are okay just delays the pain that *will* demand to be felt.
Grief that's buried alive doesn't die—it just festers in the dark. You don't have to hold it all alone.
Not anymore.

THE RISE BACK TAKEAWAY:

When the casseroles stop coming and the world moves on,
you're still left holding the weight of what happened.
Don't carry it alone.
Find a peer-led suicide loss support group (people who *get it*
because they have *lived it*) or connect with a trauma-
informed counselor who will not flinch when you speak the
hard truths. Find an activity where you can create meaning
from the loss instead of trying to find meaning in the
death.
You don't need to be fixed. You need to be *heard*.
When survival turns into silence, don't let shame win. Let
connection pull you back.

TRANSFORMATION PROMPT:

Describe the difference between how you are surviving today and
how you want to live tomorrow.

_____

_____

_____

_____

_____

Silence and strength

kept you standing,

but truth reminds you

that you are worthy.

Chapter Five

ANOTHER HOLE, SAME HEART

rief doesn't keep score, and it definitely doesn't care how much you have already survived. When it comes for you, it just rips through whatever pieces you managed to patch together. This chapter is about my brother. He was gritty, tough, bossy, and completely unfiltered. If you recall, I mentioned in Chapter 2 that I hoped I would never feel that same hollow, empty feeling again—well, here it is once more.

My brother left home the minute he turned eighteen and became a paramedic. That was his calling, his passion: emergency scenes, horrific accidents, and the kind of sights no human should have to witness. Later in life, he became a safety officer on oil rigs all over the world, which meant he was the guy responsible for keeping an entire crew alive.

As a safety officer, he called the shots when things went sideways. He ran drills, investigated injuries, enforced rules, and made sure no one walked into danger on his watch. It wasn't a job for the faint of heart, and he was anything but. He had zero patience for carelessness and zero fear when it came to doing the hard things. He never got married or had kids. He was single and liked it that way. Small talk wasn't his style, nor were filters. He didn't care if what he said made others uncomfortable. If it was true, he said it. He was truly one of a kind.

He didn't walk into a room to light it up or charm anyone. He was blunt, brutally honest, and unapologetically direct. You always knew exactly where you stood with him, whether you wanted to or not. I once thought of him as the Marlboro Man, tough and rugged. He was the kind of man you imagined would live forever simply out of sheer grit and stubbornness. He was my annoying, overbearing big brother who made it his life's mission to torment me and my sister. He annoyed the hell out of us, but we knew, without question, that if anyone ever messed with us, they would have to answer to him.

Most of his adult life was spent working in remote places that I had to google just to figure out where they were. He took pride in his work and was very good at it. He would go overseas for months at a time on contracts, then come home for a couple of months. His home base was in Kerrville, Texas, about six hours from where I live.

But his heart belonged to a little stretch of land in Junction, Texas. When he came home, he would split his time between the two houses, but his focus was on building his ranch house in Junction. He spent his life savings on that ranch, building the perfect house and barn. It wasn't flashy or fancy. It was simply a place to hang his hat after his overseas work. That ranch was his sanctuary —no luxury designs, just a place where he could sit on the porch, feed his wild game, fill the pond with fish, and drink a cold beer with the wide Texas sky above him. That place was his slice of heaven, and it eventually became my whole family's slice of heaven. We would spend Thanksgiving and Christmas there, and my kids grew up there.

While he was overseas, he would call me at least twice a week. Sometimes, we would talk for ten minutes, and other times, he would simply say, "I am alive. Are you good?" That was his way of checking in.

In January 2019, my brother flew to India for what would be his last contract. He was thrilled about this one, very happy to have secured the contract. The vessel was the *Audacia*, a massive Dutch pipe-laying ship out of the Kakinada Port, right off the Bay of Bengal. He knew it was a damn good gig: high stakes, high pay, and the kind of work he had mastered over the decades.

In June of that year, he called me from Uppada, a small coastal village in Andhra Pradesh, India, and said, "Man, I don't feel good. I haven't felt good for a couple of weeks. I think I ate some bad curry or prawns, and I might have food poisoning. It just isn't going away." I asked if there was a doctor nearby, but he was in such a rural area of India that there wasn't anywhere close he could go. He decided to fly home to see a doctor, since his contract was almost up anyway.

Once he got home, he went straight to the ER. He called me the day before I was about to leave for a dear friend's wedding in Punta Cana and said, "I just left the ER. They took a bunch of scans, and it's pancreatic cancer." He told me this with no emotion, not even flinching. He simply stated the facts, explaining that he would start chemo and fight it as hard as he could, treating it like a challenge he planned to conquer. He never even entertained the idea that he might not beat it, and neither did I. Denial is such a powerful drug—almost as strong as the vodka I would spend the next week drowning in.

My husband and I flew out the next morning for Punta Cana. I drank for a week straight, smiled in all the photos, and toasted at the wedding, but inside, I was completely shattered. I pushed my feelings aside because I didn't know how to process them. Instead, I drank them, downing every bit of vodka I could get my hands on. Every morning, I woke up with a hangover and a pit in my stomach. Every night, I numbed the pain again. I didn't cry, talk, or feel... I drank.

He had asked me not to tell my sister, as he didn't want her to know yet, only because he knew she would freak out. Keeping something that big from her felt impossible. My sister and I are incredibly close, just eighteen months apart. Our mom dressed us the same when we were younger, and everyone thought we were twins. So, keeping that secret from her was hard. I finally ended up telling her. I had to. She is my best friend, my mirror, my other half. Then I said, "Don't tell Shane I told you." That week, somewhere deep down, past the vodka and denial and celebration, I felt it, a quiet voice whispering, *This is not going to end the way you think it will.*

As my brother began his chemo, the decline came fast. The doctors gave him a year to live. My sister quit her job to move there and take care of him, feed him, take him to chemo, and do anything else he needed. My son, who had started college about an hour and a half away, would visit him on weekends. They shared an undeniable bond. My son was the only boy in the family, surrounded by girls, so they really connected.

I would drive six hours to see my brother every other week. I just couldn't stay away. During those visits, we would go to the ranch, where we would fill the feeders, put out hay for the deer, swap out dead batteries in the game cameras, and fill the pond with fish. He and my sister fished a lot on the pond at the ranch during that time. The silence out there was never heavy. It was healing in its own quiet way. I think being out there on the ranch gave him a feeling of control as everything else started slipping away, including his appetite, strength, and sense of time.

Once the chemo started, his body began to fail. He dropped to about 105 pounds. He had always been a burly 225-pound man, so the change was shocking.

One night, my sister and I were there, and his paramedic instincts kicked in, and he said, "I think I need to go to the hospital. Something's not right." So, we went to the emergency room.

The tumor on his pancreas had grown significantly, and there was nothing more they could do for him. He stayed in the hospital for a few days, and then we brought him home on hospice care. He lasted maybe another four days. We were all there as the end drew closer: my sister, my niece and nephew, my husband, my son, and Thomas, my brother's right-hand man on the ranch. Thomas lived with my brother and thought of him as a son.

My brother was in and out of reality due to the heavy pain medication while in hospice. One night, he sat up straight in bed, looked at me with a serious expression, and asked, "Am I dying?" It caught me off guard, and I didn't know what to say. He kept looking at me and asking me if he was dying, and I knew I had to tell him the truth, which broke my heart. So, I said yes, and right after that, he slipped into a delusion, thinking he was Billy the Kid. Thankfully, those drugs helped him not fully grasp reality.

He passed away on November 10, 2019, and we were all there, holding his hand and showering him with love as he took his last breath. The doctors gave him a year to live, and he lasted six months. My sister completely lost it. Her sobs were the kind that shake the whole house. My son was nineteen years old when my brother died. He had grown up so much by then, and he was the strong one. He comforted me and my sister until the funeral home came to get my brother's body and until we both fell asleep. I remember thinking what a great kid we raised.

I know my son misses his uncle so much. They were so close over the years. I think it became an unspoken agreement between my son and me... don't bring it up unless you are ready to fall apart. Neither of us was ready to talk about my brother for a while. He knew that if we did, I would break down.

After my brother was cremated, my sister and I drove his ashes home. We held the funeral back in our hometown. The room was filled with old friends, fellow medics, and people who knew him from his wild days and his heroic ones. I am grateful that we even got to have the funeral because in March 2020, COVID hit, and funerals didn't happen. He got the goodbye he deserved.

After the funeral, we went to the bar, which, I suppose, is what people do to celebrate someone's life, right? We laughed, cried, and shared stories about him because he really was larger than life and impossible to forget. It felt like the right thing to do, to raise a glass in his name.

That night, I think I crossed a line I didn't fully see at the time. Drinking stopped being something I did to take the edge off, and I started drinking to escape and avoid feeling anything, to simply survive. Losing my brother shattered me and my sister. There was the crushing reality that we are the last two members left of our family.

I had already been in survival mode for nearly a decade after losing my parents, but my brother's death pushed me over the edge, to a place I didn't know how to climb out of. I didn't know how to handle such overwhelming grief. I started drinking more. It wasn't every day, but when I did drink, it was to feel nothing. I was still working, parenting, and smiling when I needed to, but inside, I was disappearing. Drinking made it easier to disappear, and the pain got quieter, but unfortunately, so did I.

In 2020, I quit CrossFit, a place I had turned to for therapy during the past twelve years. My hip was starting to hurt, but it wasn't just physical pain—everything else, including my emotional state, hurt. Grief drained the joy from my movement. I didn't want to lift weights anymore because the burden of my grief felt heavier than the weight I was lifting.

When my brother died, I didn't ask for time off. I didn't fall apart at my desk. I just kept moving like nothing had happened. My boss was incredibly supportive and kind, but she was also a workaholic. I wasn't about to be the one who cracked under pressure, so I matched her energy no matter the cost. Six weeks after my brother's last breath, we were knee-deep in tax season. I was shattered and hollow, still pretending. Grief had no place on my calendar, so I buried it under tax returns and deadlines, hoping that if I stayed busy enough, I wouldn't have to feel.

As the executor of my brother's estate, I also buried myself in paperwork and property decisions for two years, telling myself I didn't have time to fall apart. I allowed myself to avoid every single emotion that was begging to be felt. But grief doesn't just disappear—it sits and waits.

This was a tough chapter to write. I cried through most of it. I went down the rabbit hole of looking at his Facebook page for hours. Losing my brother broke something in me that I didn't know was still fragile. I thought I had survived the worst with my parents, but this was different. I don't think I realized how much I had been avoiding this grief until I sat down to write this chapter. Maybe this is the beginning of finally letting myself process his death.

I don't know what I would have done without my sister during all of this. We have walked through the losses of our mom, dad, and brother side by side, and our relationship has never wavered. We are the only two left from the family we were born into, and that kind of survival creates an unshakable bond. She draws strength from me while I draw strength from her.

We don't talk much about the deaths. Not because we don't feel them, but because we feel them too much. It's a weight we both carry quietly, only speaking of it when absolutely necessary, and even then, we tread lightly. Shared grief has its own language, and somehow, we both know it.

In a world that keeps taking, I am endlessly grateful that I still have her.

A SURVIVOR'S TRUTH:

Avoiding your grief doesn't mean you are healing—it means you are surviving on autopilot. I buried myself in paperwork, responsibilities, and tasks because it felt easier than facing what was underneath. But grief doesn't disappear just because you delay it. It waits. It lingers. And it will demand to be felt. You can't outwork, outrun, or outdrink the pain. You have to slow down, feel it, and let safe people in.

THE RISE BACK TAKEAWAY:

Don't isolate yourself. Grief wants to pull you inward, but healing happens in a safe community. Find people who will sit with you—not fix you. Your pain deserves a place to land.

On the days when the weight feels like too much, try this:

- **Move your body:** a walk, a stretch, or just stepping outside. You don't have to run a marathon. You just have to *move.*
- **Breathe with intention:** in through your nose for a count of four, hold for four, out through your mouth for six. Repeat until your body softens.
- **Journal the truth:** No filters, no structure. Just empty the storm onto the page.
- **Ground yourself:** Use the 5-4-3-2-1 technique: Name five things you can see, four you can touch, three you can hear, two you can smell, and one you can taste.
- **Drink water before wine.** You don't have to be perfect. Just be aware. Your body is already carrying so much—you need to hydrate it.
- **Speak the name of your person out loud.** Tell a story about them. Laugh. Cry. Let their memory live. You have the right to hold on to the love and good memories of the one you lost, no matter what happened before or during their final moments.

This is not about healing overnight. It's about creating a moment of peace in the middle of the chaos. Show up for yourself every single day.

TRANSFORMATION PROMPT:

What have you been using to numb your pain? Write about how it has helped you survive—and what it has cost you.

_____

_____

_____

_____

_____

You are not starting over,

You are starting from strength.

Using every scar, every lesson,

and every tool life gave you.

This moment was made for the

version of you who survived.

Chapter Six

WHERE THE BROKEN FIND THE BRAVE

*I*n 2020, I was watching the news when a sweet girl appeared on TV to discuss the creation of a LOSS team in my town. She explained what it was and invited anyone who was a survivor of suicide loss to reach out and volunteer to be on the team.

I felt a surge of excitement, as it was the first time in a decade that I had felt truly human, like a brave, broken-hearted individual carrying invisible wounds. I had survived alone for far too long. Joining the team has allowed me to meet other survivors, and together, we help others navigate the worst day of their lives.

So, what is the LOSS team? As I detailed in the Introduction, LOSS stands for Local Outreach to Suicide Survivors. It consists of survivors of suicide loss (people who have experienced it), along with first responders and mental health professionals trained to provide support after a suicide has occurred.

Our mission is simple yet profound: no one should have to face the aftermath of suicide alone. We sign up to be on call for as much or as little time as we want. When we get a call, our goal is to arrive on the scene of a suicide within fifteen minutes to help the loved ones left behind get through the most devastating moments.

Our support is both practical and personal. We provide survivors with a binder filled with essential information like how to write an obituary, who to call for scene restoration, and where to find immediate resources. But we also step in to meet real needs in the moment. Sometimes that looks like letting the dog outside, making phone calls no one has the strength to make, or finding a hotel room so a family member has somewhere to sleep. Other times, it's more intimate: holding back someone's hair while they are sick, pressing a cool washcloth to their forehead, or rocking and feeding a baby so a grieving parent can catch their breath. These are not small things. They are the lifelines that help people survive those first unbearable hours after losing someone to suicide.

When a loved one dies by suicide, the LOSS team is dispatched to the scene, not to fix things, preach, or analyze, but simply to be present. We offer resources and a comforting presence, providing an understanding that only those who have experienced similar loss can offer. Typically, two people arrive on scene: a survivor like me and a trained mental health professional. Together, we step into the unthinkable.

We serve as a bridge between the police and the family, helping to answer questions and keep communication clear during those first chaotic hours. When I lost both of my parents, that kind of support didn't exist. We were not guided. We were simply left in the dark. Things have changed since then. Now, I have seen first-hand how compassionate and human law enforcement can be when they understand that supporting the family is just as important as processing the scene. This is what postvention looks like in real time: trauma-informed, survivor-led, and human.

"Postvention" is the organized support that happens after a suicide, created to help survivors through those first raw hours and days, so they are not left alone in the dark like I was.

The LOSS team's model was developed by Dr. Frank Campbell in 1998 at the Baton Rouge Crisis and Trauma Center. He introduced the active postvention model to address the critical need for immediate support for suicide loss survivors. Dr. Campbell recognized that, on average, it took survivors around four and a half years to seek help, a period during which many suffered in silence and developed unhealthy coping mechanisms, including self-medicating with alcohol.

The LOSS team aims to bridge this gap by providing compassionate support immediately following a suicide loss, with the hope of reducing the average time before someone seeks help from four and a half years to about four and a half months. If someone is ready for it, we also offer therapy to support their healing journey. The peer-based approach ensures that at least one volunteer has personally experienced a loss due to suicide, which provides a unique and empathetic perspective.

Most survivors don't seek help right away, not because we don't want to, but because the shame is so loud. The stigma and the weight of it all are silencing. Lack of awareness about available resources comes into play. There is also emotional paralysis, where the pain is so overwhelming that taking that first step feels impossible. Understanding these statistics is not just about understanding the numbers. It's about recognizing the patterns that many, including myself, fall into. Self-medicating is a very common, although unhealthy, coping mechanism. Delayed help-seeking is not a sign of weakness but a reflection of the complex nature of grief.

When I joined the LOSS team, I realized for the first time that I wasn't crazy for still feeling pain—I was just human. If I had had someone like this when my parents took their lives, maybe I wouldn't have bottled everything up or drowned in silence. Maybe I would have healed sooner. Or maybe not? Who knows? Maybe my path unfolded exactly as it had to be. I will never know, but here is what I do know: God has used my pain for a purpose.

Once I found the LOSS team, I felt in my bones that I couldn't remain trapped in my own story any longer. I had to step into someone else's. So, I trained, showed up, and eventually became part of something I desperately needed: a lifeline for the newly bereaved. Now I see my younger self in the dazed eyes of a woman who just lost her mother or the trembling hands of a teenager who just found his dad. I don't offer advice. I just provide my presence because I know how it feels when no one shows up.

I have always had a passion for helping people. In college, I got my degree in criminal justice because I was fascinated by the human mind and dreamed of becoming a criminal psychologist. But in my small town, those jobs didn't exist. So right out of college, I got a job as a juvenile probation officer, and then I became a parole officer and stayed at that job until my son was born. Helping others has always been in my blood.

Being part of the LOSS team has shown me that serving doesn't mean you have it all figured out. It means you are brave enough to let your brokenness become someone else's lifeline. That matters, because research shows suicide loss survivors are *seven times* more likely to die by suicide themselves. That's not just a number—it's a warning.

Authentic, soul-level community opens the door to hope, and this part is crucial. You need people who get it. Not just therapists, but other survivors who understand the silence, the questions, and the weight of it. Start by looking for peer-led groups or suicide loss communities in your area. Many are out there, both online and in person, and your local LOSS team can often help you find them.

And if you can't find one, create one. Healing doesn't need a big stage. It just needs a safe space, a few chairs, or even a Zoom link. Healing begins in shared silence, in witnessed pain, in the simple act of showing up together.

Grieving a suicide loss is not like grieving any other kind of death. It's complicated, heavy, and far-reaching. Dr. Campbell describes it as a **ripple effect**—when someone dies by suicide, the devastation stretches far beyond the casket. Research shows that, on average, 135 people are directly impacted by one suicide. This includes family members, friends, coworkers, neighbors, classmates, teachers, first responders, and even acquaintances who barely knew them.

These individuals are often left grappling with a loss that feels incomprehensible. About one in five will carry that loss like an open wound, experiencing deep emotional and psychological consequences that can persist for years. For around six of those people, the grief is life-shattering. In the U.S. alone, with more than 49,000 suicide deaths each year, that translates to approximately 6.6 million people impacted annually, with over a million struggling to function under the weight of their loss.

This is why I keep showing up. It's why I keep writing, speaking, and sharing my story even when it's hard. Suicide is the only kind of death that can feel like a homicide without a killer—sudden, violent, and leaving you desperate for someone to blame. It leaves behind devastation, unanswered questions, and chaos that touches everyone connected to the person. It shatters so many lives. It's like a silent explosion that no one saw coming. That's why suicide postvention isn't optional—it's lifesaving. Postvention *is* prevention.

The most recent statistics that we have on suicides are from 2023, and that data is still provisional, which means the final count may be even higher. We will not see the 2024 report for a little while, but we do know the numbers are still rising.

In 2023, almost 50,000 people in the U.S. died by suicide. That's one person gone every eleven minutes. The numbers behind the deaths are staggering. In 2022, an estimated 12.8 million adults seriously considered suicide, 3.7 million made a plan, and 1.5 million attempted.

Suicide affects people of every age. In 2023, it ranked among the top eight leading causes of death for people ages ten to sixty-four, and it was the second leading cause of death for those ages ten to thirty-four. This is not just a problem—it's an emergency. Sometimes, I think we forget that these numbers are people: someone's son, daughter, best friend, parent, or spouse. They had stories, dreams, pain, and worth. They mattered.

Men account for almost eighty percent of suicide deaths, not because they are hurting more, but because they are told to hurt less, to be tough, to keep it all in. That silence turns into something dangerous. Women are more likely to attempt suicide, more likely to think about it, and more likely to keep pushing through the pain while wearing a smile.

And let's not forget about our veterans. According to the VA, around seventeen to eighteen veterans die by suicide every single day. Some independent research suggests it could be more than forty a day when you count overdose and self-harm deaths. That's one life lost every eighty-two minutes. It's heartbreaking and unacceptable, and that number is rising.

Firearms remain the leading method of suicide in the U.S. The tragedy is their finality. With firearms, there is almost no chance to change your mind. They are fast, fatal, and irreversible.

Survivors are part of a heartbreaking group that nobody wants to join, and it's an issue the world still struggles to discuss. I didn't join the LOSS team because I had it all figured out. I joined because I remember what it felt like to be all alone with no safe place to fall apart, ask questions, or have someone tell me, "You are not alone."

I am a survivor who shows up for survivors, and I do it because I know what silence can steal. Every time we speak the truth, we can chip away at the shame and remind someone that their pain is survivable. I believe healing begins the moment someone feels seen. We have to say the hard things out loud. As long as we keep showing up, again and again, silence doesn't get the last word.

IF YOU ARE STRUGGLING OR HAVE LOST SOMEONE TO SUICIDE, PLEASE KNOW YOU ARE NOT ALONE:

988 Suicide & Crisis Lifeline
Call or Text **988**
Available 24/7 for anyone experiencing a mental health crisis, thoughts of suicide, or emotional distress—including suicide loss survivors.
www.988lifeline.org

Crisis Text Line
Text **HELLO** to **741741**
Free, 24/7, confidential support via text from trained crisis counselors.
www.crisistextline.org

NAMI (National Alliance on Mental Illness) Helpline
Call **1-800-950-NAMI (6264)** or Text **"HelpLine" to 62640**
Monday–Friday, 10 a.m.–10 p.m. ET
Answers questions about mental health conditions, treatment options, and local support.
www.nami.org/help

Alliance of Hope for Suicide Loss Survivors
Online community and resources for those grieving a suicide loss.
www.allianceofhope.org

American Foundation for Suicide Prevention (AFSP)

Resources for loss survivors, support groups, and healing tools.

www.afsp.org

Find a LOSS Team Near You

The LOSS Team (Local Outreach to Suicide Survivors) provides in-person support in many areas. To locate one in your community, visit:

www.lossteam.com

You don't have to walk this path alone. Reach out. Speak up. Healing begins with connection.

A SURVIVOR'S TRUTH:

You don't have to be healed to help.

Sometimes, the bravest thing you can do is show up exactly as you are and reach for connection anyway.

Isolation feeds the pain.

But community, real, honest, soul-level community, cracks the door open for hope.

THE RISE BACK TAKEAWAY:

Stop waiting until you feel "better" to plug back into life.
Join a peer-led grief support group.
Volunteer for a cause that touches your story.

Start a weekly coffee date with someone who gets it.
Find a way to serve that also helps you stay connected.
This is how we rise, not by going it alone but by walking
each other home.

TRANSFORMATION PROMPT:

Who do you need to reach out to—or finally let in—so you don't
keep carrying this alone?

_____

_____

_____

_____

_____

Sometimes, we don't need the bright side. We just need people to sit with us in the pain. Learning to hold space for each other in hard moments is one of the most human things we can do.

Chapter Seven

WHEN THE NOISE FADES, THE GRIEF SPEAKS

I wasn't healed. I was just busy. And when the noise stopped, the heartbreak echoed louder than ever.

In 2021, my daughter graduated from high school, and we packed her up and moved her to college five and a half hours away. In her first week there, she contracted COVID and had to isolate for ten days. It was a crazy time, and my anxiety was through the roof.

A few weeks later, we packed up a U-Haul and moved my son across the country to North Carolina, where he was starting a new job. I was so incredibly proud of both of them. They were thriving and chasing their dreams, and it was a true "proud mom" moment.

My husband and I thought we were ready for the kids to be out of the house. We looked forward to becoming empty nesters. We told ourselves, *We did it... We raised good humans, and they are off chasing their dreams. This is the next chapter.*

It was supposed to be exciting, but no one tells you how brutal the silence can be when that noise was your whole identity. The house got too quiet. No more chaos, no more laughter. I used to complain about the chaos, but once the kids were both gone, I would have given anything to have it back. Being a mom wasn't just part of me—it was *all* of me. It was who I was, my purpose, my reason. When that part of life faded, it felt like someone had ripped out a piece of my soul. I didn't know who I was without the chaos.

I continued working through COVID, as I was deemed essential since I was an accountant, but the world outside had shut down, and so had all my distractions. The grief I thought I had outrun was waiting for me in this silence. I wasn't just grieving the change. I was grieving *me*. The version of me I had known for almost two decades no longer existed.

I wasn't ready for this change. I had been so involved in my kids' lives, and their lives had become mine. My kids saved me all those years without even realizing it. They kept me anchored, needed, and were my reason to hold it together. My husband was still traveling for work every other week, which only amplified my loneliness and emptiness. I know he was doing what he had to do, but it felt like abandonment every time, like everyone had moved on but me.

I felt lost and lonely, and it hit me hard. I didn't want to sit in that loneliness, so I drank. By that time, even the alcohol couldn't take the edge off of what I was starting to feel. There was a heaviness I couldn't explain, a true soul ache. It wasn't sadness or stress —it was something much deeper. For the first time, I realized what it was: *grief.*

For years, I had been too busy, too distracted, and too needed by everyone else to feel it. Now that things at home were quiet, it finally caught up to me. But in true Tiff fashion, I still wasn't ready to deal with it, so I drank more. I wasn't an everyday drinker, but when I did drink, I binged hard. I wasn't drinking to enjoy myself. I was drinking to escape myself, to black out, to silence the deep ache in my chest.

It was ugly, and there is nothing worse than waking up the next morning with a pit in your stomach, wondering what you said, what you did, or who you hurt. I will never forget that shame, that sick feeling in my gut. My version of casual drinking looked a lot more like blackouts and regret.

My best friend, the same one who rode his motorcycle to my dad's house all those years ago, has always understood me. He knows every detail of my journey, and he has been my ride-or-die ever since. We have been through everything together, and he is still the one who shows up no matter what. He has never judged me or asked questions—he just lets me be messy. In 2022, his world changed when he had a life-altering stroke.

My husband and I helped him recover, and it gave me a new sense of purpose, but through it all, I still drank. I am not sure how either of them put up with me during that time, but they did. I am not sure how *anyone* put up with me during that time. I was a complete mess, a high-functioning disaster. I never missed a day of work, but that didn't mean I was okay. In fact, I was far from it. Even in that season of helping my best friend, I still couldn't shake the heaviness in my soul. It followed me everywhere: work, bed, every empty glass. Grief was quietly waiting for me to sober up long enough to face it.

I found myself crying more than usual, and that's saying something because I *never* cry. My husband used to joke that if I ever cried, it was time to run, and he wasn't wrong. I had always kept it all in. Emotions made me feel weak and out of control. My boss says that tears clear all the cobwebs out of your soul, but I was so afraid that if I let the tears flow, they might not ever stop.

Some might call my behavior survival. Others might call it self-destruction. It was probably a mix of both. Deep down, I knew I wasn't being the best version of myself, and that realization tugged at me constantly. I didn't know how to change my situation or break free from my drinking routine.

That first sip, that first burn in my chest, felt like relief. For a moment, everything softened. I could breathe. But the relief never lasted. It was a trap that only made the chaos louder. I was always in overdrive (over-giving, overthinking, people-pleasing), and I didn't know how to slow down or sit alone with myself.

Despite everything I did to stay numb, my soul ached for more. I couldn't name it then, but I could feel it. I knew I was meant for more than just functioning, I just didn't know how to get there. Instead, I was miserable, unfulfilled, and to top it all off, my health was unraveling. I was running out of ways to outrun myself.

I felt terrible all the time—exhausted, foggy, heavy. Blood work showed I was severely anemic. I needed two iron infusions, was prescribed cholesterol meds, and had to add another blood pressure pill to the one I was already taking. I was still on trazodone just to sleep. My stomach hurt, my energy was gone, and the headaches never stopped. My body was falling apart, and I couldn't make sense of it. Deep down, I knew the drinking was wrecking me, but I also didn't realize how much trauma was showing up in my body, too.

The troubling part was that no doctor ever asked about my lifestyle—they just handed me more pills. I was becoming a walking pharmacy. No one mentioned grief or trauma or suggested looking deeper. Honestly, I didn't want to, either, because facing those realities meant confronting things I wasn't ready for. So I kept pushing through, exhausted, foggy, and in pain, wondering what was happening to me while knowing, deep down, something bigger was at play.

I thought I was broken beyond repair, like my emotions had just shut down. Even though I had learned mental health CPR through the LOSS team, I never once applied it to myself. I kept showing up for others in their darkest moments, walking into homes where life had just been split into a "before" and an "after." The work was sacred, but it was also soul-draining. The calls kept getting harder and heavier, and I couldn't shake the sadness after a suicide call.

I knew something had to change. What I didn't realize was that I had been living in a full-blown trauma response for years on top of numbing with alcohol, piling grief on top of stress, then stepping into suicide calls as if I was indestructible. Nobody told me that grief, stress, alcohol, and shame can trap your nervous system in fight, flight, or freeze. Time doesn't heal that on its own. I didn't need another pill. I needed a way to reset my nervous system from the inside out. That's when I began creating what I now call my "Soul Reset Routine."

I started this routine slowly. I didn't do everything perfectly. Some days, I barely got through one thing. If your soul is aching, this might be the place for you to start. Little by little, maybe this routine will help you start your healing process.

My Soul Reset Routine:

1. **Stillness Before Screens:**
   Five minutes of silence, prayer, or deep breathing before I touch my phone. I let my soul speak before the world does.

2. **Truth-Telling Journal:**
   One page a day. First, I write 3 things I am grateful for, 3 truths I know today, and 3 wins (even the tiniest ones). Then I ask myself: What am I feeling? What am I avoiding? What do I need today? Be honest.

3. **Nervous System Support:**
   A cold-water splash to wake up, a weighted-vest walk, or a few stretches to remind my body I am still here. A few deep breaths until I feel myself settle back into my body.

4. **Hydration + Nutrition:**
   Water before coffee, every time. Eat to support, not punish, your body.

5. **One Act of Connection:**
   Text someone. Ask for help. Let someone in. Shame dies in safe connections.

6. **Soulful Soundtrack:**
   Listen to music that matches your mood, or shifts it. Let it move you, literally.

A SURVIVOR'S TRUTH:

You are tired and frustrated, and you don't know why. You sleep. You eat "okay." You go through the motions. But something still feels off.

It's your nervous system still stuck in survival mode.

High cortisol. Low repair. Constant vigilance.

You didn't fail. Your body is doing exactly what it was trained to do: protect you from more pain. But you can't live a full life in a state of emergency.

Your healing starts when you stop blaming your body—and start listening to it.

THE RISE BACK TAKEAWAY:

Your pain deserves a name, and your healing deserves intention. Speak your pain. Then start rewriting your strength.

Here is how:

- Start with radical self-awareness. Keep a "trigger tracker" for one week. Write down what sets you off emotionally or physically: conversations, people, memories, silence. You can't heal what you won't name.
- Detox your habits, not just your body. If your go-to comfort is a drink, a scroll, or another distraction, replace it, even once. Try movement, cold water, breathwork, or blasting music that makes you feel again.
- Get your hands on your healing. Therapy is one tool, but so is breathwork, art, writing, screaming in the car, and grounding in the grass. Don't wait for permission. Healing is messy and loud. Experiment until something shifts.
- Create a sacred routine that's just for you. Call it your soul reset routine: fifteen minutes a day of truth-telling,

stillness, or sweat. Your healing doesn't have to be pretty, and it doesn't have to look like anyone else's.

- Say the hard thing out loud, to one person, even if it cracks your voice. Connection kills shame. Shame thrives in silence.

This is not about being perfect. It's about choosing one bold step back to yourself. Healing doesn't happen *to* you. It starts *with* you. It's an inside job.

TRANSFORMATION PROMPT:

What part of yourself have you abandoned that you are ready to welcome home?

_____

_____

_____

_____

_____

A step back is not failure.

It's preparation.

This is the part where you

catch your breath,

clear your mind,

and steady your heart.

The next part of your journey

deserves a stronger you.

Chapter Eight

THE CUT THAT NEVER HEALED

*A*fter suffering from hip pain for three long years, I was finally diagnosed with a torn labrum in my left hip in 2024. I suspect that it was a result of my years of doing CrossFit and my years of playing tennis. I played tennis right up until I had surgery. Luckily, steroid injections got me through the pain, along with physical therapy. Insurance made me jump through every hoop before approving me for surgery. I had started my Soul Reset Routine, little by little, and I was starting to feel human again. I thought I was finally finding ways to quiet the chaos, but my body had other plans. The pain was about to take me down in ways I never saw coming.

When I met with the surgeon, he briefly prepared me for the procedure and mentioned that recovery could take up to a year. He explained that at my age, fifty, the labral tear repair was comparable to stitching together two pieces of wet toilet paper. As we age, cartilage becomes more fragile and less likely to hold sutures well. This meant that keeping the stitch intact could be quite challenging. By this time, I was running on empty and needed something to change. I was desperate for something to work.

Surgery day came on October 3, 2024. Two and a half hours later, I woke groggy from anesthesia. My husband explained what the surgeon had told him: they had tried to repair the labrum but couldn't stitch it back together. Instead, I learned I had femoroacetabular impingement (FAI), where the femoral head rubs abnormally against the hip socket, tearing the labrum again and again. To "fix" it, the surgeon shaved down the femoral head. So basically, the surgery was unsuccessful.

When my husband explained it, I was stunned. "Wait, what? They didn't fix it?" No one really explained what that meant. Later, when I did my own research, I discovered that osteoplasty is literally bone remodeling. And here is the thing: bone is alive. It has nerves, blood vessels, and it carries pain signals just like soft tissue. Shaving it leaves the bone raw and inflamed, which causes deep pain that is not easy to control. On top of that, the hip is surrounded by major nerves—the femoral, obturator, and sciatic— and the traction used to separate the joint during surgery can irritate or compress them, leading to excruciating nerve pain.

I spent one night in the hospital, where they kept me medicated and pain-free, before they sent me home in a massive hip brace that seemed more suited for a linebacker, not a five-foot-tall woman. I left with crutches, strict orders to stay off my feet for two weeks, and no idea of the storm that was coming.

My mother-in-law stayed with me during the first week because my husband was traveling for work and would be gone for the next five weeks, only coming home on weekends. I was truly grateful for her. She fed me, helped me with my showers, did laundry, and even tucked me in bed like I was a kid again. I needed the help, even if I didn't want to admit how helpless I felt.

However, on the second day after surgery, the nerve block wore off. I expected pain in my hip, but this was different. This pain was in my feet. It was like a creeping fire that exploded into an inferno. My God, the pain—it felt like my feet had been caught in a boat motor, chewed up, shredded, and spit out. It was like knives slicing through the bottom of my feet over and over, like open wounds exposed to salt and air, especially underneath my toes and the tips of my toes.

I kept looking at them, fully expecting to see mangled flesh. Sometimes, they looked normal, and sometimes, they were fire red, blue, purple, and swollen. The big toe on my right foot was the worst. It felt like someone was driving a nail straight through its tip, slowly, cruelly, and precisely.

This pain made me question reality. I wondered if I was dying or just going insane. At first, it was both feet, a full-blown electrical storm firing off under my skin. I couldn't sleep, I couldn't even think. No amount of pain meds even touched it. Nothing relieved the agony. I was sent home after surgery with OxyContin, tramadol, and a muscle relaxer. I took them all, but nothing helped. This wasn't typical surgical pain. It was like my nervous system had flipped a switch that I couldn't turn off. It was the most excruciating pain I had ever felt, and I had no idea what was happening to me. This was on top of the hip pain from the surgery.

Everything I did, from using the bathroom to getting into bed, was an exhausting ordeal. I was helpless and trapped in a body that felt like it had turned against me, and I had no idea why. Remember how I said that grief just sits and waits? That it festers in the silence, hides in the corners of your body, and waits for its moment? Well... this was it.

The pain wasn't just excruciating—it was relentless. All day, all night, every single day. No breaks. No days off. My surgery was on a Thursday, and by Sunday, I called the surgeon's office. The doctor on call said it might be my back causing the issue and suggested I get an MRI. He explained that the way they position patients during hip surgery can sometimes strain the back, and something might be pressing on a nerve. He advised me to go to the ER for an MRI.

At the end of the call, the doctor said, "I don't prescribe narcotics on weekends." What? I hadn't even asked for any. I still had what was prescribed after surgery, and it wasn't working. I wasn't drug seeking. He did call in gabapentin, though, and told me to start taking 300 mg three times a day, and I could go up to 3,200 mg without harming myself. Are you kidding me? It didn't even touch the pain, and the side effects were awful. I knew it would take time to work, but I couldn't stand the side effects long enough to give it time.

The most common side effects are dizziness (one of the most reported, it feels like the room is tilting or you are on a boat), extreme fatigue/sedation (many describe it as zombie mode or feeling heavily drugged), brain fog (trouble concentrating, memory lapses, or just feeling mentally off), balance issues/unsteadiness, blurred vision, nausea, swelling in the hands and feet (which I already had in my feet), mood changes (some report increased anxiety, depression, or feeling emotionally flat), tingling/numbness (it can sometimes make nerve symptoms worse before, or if, they get better), weight gain/increased appetite, and sleep issues (can either knock you out or cause insomnia in some).

Rare but serious side effects are suicidal thoughts (black box warning), allergic reactions or rashes, difficulty breathing, and severe emotional instability. A lot of people, including me, feel like they are losing their grip on reality in the early days of gabapentin. The side effects of this drug can mimic a mental breakdown, causing dizziness, dissociation, emotional numbness, and a haunting sense that your thoughts are no longer safe. Doesn't that sound pleasant? Not to mention, it did nothing to help with the pain.

I went back to see my surgeon when he returned to the office. Thankfully, my best friend, who had suffered a stroke, drove me to all my doctor appointments, out to eat, to pick up medications, and even to work, as I wasn't allowed to drive for six weeks. I was on crutches, and he was one-handed with a cane—it was like the blind leading the blind, but we made it work.

When I finally met with my surgeon, he prescribed me a steroid to take for two weeks. He hoped it would help with the inflammation, and he told me to increase the dosage of the gabapentin. He wasn't sure what was going on, but he speculated that the booties they used during surgery might have been too tight, resulting in some peripheral nerve damage. He said nerves take a really long time to heal.

I felt frustrated, and I thought, *This is not normal. People undergo hip surgeries every day without these issues.* Every doctor I saw made me feel like I was crazy. Regarding the suggestion to go to the ER for an MRI, I knew they wouldn't perform those on-site. They would have to be scheduled. Plus, I doubted I could endure the pain of getting an MRI anyway.

I upped the dosage of the gabapentin, but the pain didn't budge. My feet pulsed and burned like my nerves were short-circuiting from the inside out. The higher the dose, the worse I felt. My brain was foggy, my body felt sluggish, and I was constantly sick to my stomach. I didn't feel relief—I felt numb and broken, which is a terrifying place to be.

At my four-week follow-up, I shuffled into the office wearing house shoes that were a size too big because I couldn't have anything touching my feet, and I was still on crutches. I couldn't wear socks or shoes. Even a blanket or sheet brushing against my foot sent me screaming in pain. During the checkup, my surgeon poked around but remained confused and unable to pinpoint the issue. I kept insisting that I couldn't be the only one to have this kind of pain after surgery. He eventually referred me to a pain specialist and a neurologist—I think just to shut me up.

Getting an appointment with the pain doctor took a while, so I started physical therapy three times a week for five weeks. They focused on my foot rather than my hip, as it was the main issue. The physical therapy was absolute hell. I felt like I was going to be sick every time I went. Unfortunately, it didn't help, and since my foot hurt so much, I could barely walk, which hindered any work on my hip. This meant that my hip was getting stiffer and not improving at all.

I went back to work after five weeks. My boss's husband had knee surgery the week after my surgery and ended up very sick with life-threatening complications. Even with her husband in the ICU, she would show up at my house with five bags of groceries, set them on the kitchen counter, and then head straight back to the hospital. I have no idea how we managed to keep the office running, but we got it done between the two of us, payroll and all. I was still drowning in pain and fogged out on gabapentin, and she was carrying the weight of her own crisis.

I finally got in to see the pain specialist. She took me off the gabapentin and started me on Lyrica. She told me to go home and take two Lyrica and two tramadol to relieve the pain. She stated that I had to get my pain under control because my body was starting to shut down. She also said we would worry about weaning off all of this later. I am pretty sure she could tell how miserable I was.

The fog of pain can make you susceptible to anything that promises relief, so I did exactly what she said and went to bed. I woke up in the middle of the night, but when I tried to get up, I passed out cold on the floor. I woke up feeling dazed, confused, and scared. My husband was still on the road, so I was home alone. I called my best friend the next morning and couldn't even talk. I slurred my words, my heart was racing, and I couldn't form a complete sentence. I was trying to explain what had happened, but I couldn't even get that out. Lyrica made me feel like I was drunk times one thousand (and trust me, I had been drunk before).

The next day, I called the pain doctor's office to tell them what had happened. The nurse on the phone asked, "Well, what did you take?"

"Two tramadol and two Lyrica, just like the doctor told me to," I replied.

Her tone shifted, and she said, "We never told you to take two of anything."

My best friend had been sitting right there with me during the appointment and heard her give me those exact instructions, but now they were making it sound like I had overmedicated myself, and it was my fault. The truth is, they nearly overdosed me.

I decided that I was done with Lyrica. The side effects were brutal anyway: brain fog, dizziness, that disconnected feeling like I wasn't even in my own body, feeling like I had just downed six shots of vodka. But oh my gosh, the pain was still so unbearable that I would break the capsule open and dab a little of the Lyrica powder on my tongue at night just to take the edge off so I could make it through the night. I did this for about another month. I would also take a single tramadol with it, trying to find that thin line between numbing the agony and keeping myself conscious.

Lyrica has the same side effects as gabapentin. Lyrica also carries serious mental health risks, especially for those with a personal or family history of depression or addiction. These include suicidal thoughts or behavior, mood swings, increased anxiety or panic, and emotional numbness. The doctor never even mentioned these side effects, and she especially didn't mention that combining it with tramadol could be deadly.

Every time I swallowed one of those pills, it gave me extreme anxiety, like I was on the edge of a cliff I swore I would never go near. I told my pain doctor, my surgeon, my regular doctor, anyone who would listen, that my family has a history of suicide. I needed them to understand that this was different for me—I didn't want any more pills. All they saw was me in pain, and they handed me the same prescriptions they gave my mom that eventually failed her.

I needed someone to hear my fears. The fear that I would step into the same darkness that had taken my mom. She was in pain, and the doctors kept giving her pills. When those stopped working, they gave her stronger ones. Eventually, she needed them just to feel normal, just to function, just to exist... until she didn't anymore. It was like God had given me a front-row seat to my mom's life. I was terrified of dying from trying to chase relief.

I was angry at my mom for eighteen years. Not sad, *angry*. That rage sat in my chest like a brick. I was angry that she left us, that she missed everything, that she didn't get to see her grandkids grow up to be incredible humans. I loved her so much, but I was furious that she chose to leave. All of this led me to realize that I needed to stop seeing her as the mother who had abandoned me and start seeing her as a woman in pain who had run out of options—a woman whose body and mind had been hijacked by medications, silence, and despair. When I finally laid that anger down, I started healing. It only took me eighteen years (but who's counting).

My hip was getting stiffer and not improving at all. The surgeon had referred me to a neurologist, but that doctor wouldn't see me. When I called to schedule my nerve studies, I mentioned that my doctor suspected it might be my back. The neurologist simply said, "I don't deal with backs," and refused to help.

Eventually, I went to another doctor just for nerve studies, and everything came back "normal." They told me my nerves were perfectly fine. That was just another blow. I kept thinking, *What is wrong with me? Why is my foot still hurting? This is insane.*

Through it all, I kept working. My boss was incredibly under-standing, and if I needed to leave early, I could. I was still in extreme pain, but I craved a sense of normalcy and needed to work. Ironically, that December, my boss ended up having a hip replacement, and by January, we were diving headfirst into tax season. Somehow, we made it through, and it actually turned out to be a smooth season despite everything.

My mornings were manageable, but by noon, I would experi-ence what I called the "cold burn." It felt like ice inside my leg and foot. By that time, the pain had shifted to my right foot, leaving my left foot unaffected, which was strange since it used to affect both feet. However, it wasn't on the surgery side—it was on the opposite side.

By about two o'clock, the cold burn would turn into a hot one. By the time I left work, I would be in excruciating pain. It felt like my foot was on fire as I drove home. Every time I pressed down on the accelerator, the pain was intense, like fire ants were biting my foot and leg. At the same time, electrical shocks shot down my spine and into my toes, making me wince in pain.

Nobody seemed to have any answers for me. I felt like the surgeon had given up because he eventually just referred me to the neurologist and said, "Good luck. I don't know what's going on with you."

By February, the pain was still unrelenting. Burning, stabbing, pulsing through my feet like I was walking on glass shards. I was exhausted and desperate, and the chronic fatigue had set in from my body constantly fighting the pain.

I found a holistic clinic in town. The woman there listened to me, but then charged me a ridiculous amount of money for a custom supplement protocol that I will not even go into. At that point, I would have drunk horse piss if someone promised it would help, so I paid for it. Then she invited me to join her MLM (multi-level marketing.) *What?* Thankfully, I had just enough sense left to say no.

The supplements did lower my cholesterol, but they did nothing for my pain. She kept insisting I had neuropathy and was probably diabetic, even though my labs showed otherwise. Her intentions were good, though. She tried red light therapy, a dot on my wrist that supposedly emitted healing frequencies, and even goggles that pulsed light and sound while vibrating my earlobes to "rewire" my brain around the pain. None of it touched the fire in my foot.

I poured every ounce of energy, money, and hope into chasing remedies for the pain. Nothing worked. It felt like my nervous system was stuck on fire with no off switch. The pain was there every single day—all day.

I felt dismissed by everyone, so in a last-ditch effort, I turned to a chiropractor. By then, I could barely move, let alone walk. The pain was unbearable. My psoas muscles had locked around my spine, stealing my mobility. My left hip had no range of motion. My glute and quad had stopped engaging, and every muscle meant to support my hip had given out. My sciatic nerve was lit up with pain.

My body was shutting down, and my spirit wasn't far behind. It felt like everything in me was breaking at once. I was desperate, exhausted, and hanging on by a thread. If you have ever lived with pain that never ends, you know exactly what I mean.

The chiropractor started treating me, focusing on easing the pressure from my psoas muscle, which was excruciating. My foot was so sensitive that I couldn't even let him touch it. He also suspected neuropathy, and he was the first person to suggest that this condition might not go away. That stopped me dead in my tracks. Not one doctor had ever said this could be permanent. I was stunned—it almost didn't register. Who thinks about living with pain for the rest of their life after hip surgery? I honestly believed it was temporary, so I dismissed his words and clung to the only thing I had left: hope.

I saw him three times a week, and the cost added up quickly. Since he used laser therapy on patients with neuropathy, he decided to try it on me. But during my second treatment, his staff had the machine turned up too high. I didn't know it at the time, but it fried the nerves in my foot even more. The next day, I went back and told him something was different. This was a horrible new pain, not the pain I had been living with.

I spent the next nine days in terrible pain. It felt like I had the worst sunburn of my life, like my skin had been shredded and peeled back. Even the air hurt. I had found one pair of tennis shoes that I could wear before this, extra wide and a size too big. No socks, though. The thought of socks made me sick to my stomach, and still does. After the laser incident, I couldn't even wear shoes.

I was starting to lose faith in any kind of treatment, and my body and my soul were just so tired. When I informed him about the mistake, he was understandably upset and said he would address the issue with his staff. Despite the incident, that chiropractor ultimately saved my life. He helped restore my mobility, and he was the only one who truly listened to me. I was so grateful for him.

He eventually brought a new machine into the office, something like a TENS unit but designed as a nerve regenerator. He asked me to be the guinea pig, so I took it home for thirty days, tracked my progress, and gave him feedback. This machine didn't take the pain away, but it did take the edge off, and even that felt like a small miracle.

By this time, I also think my brain started adapting, making the pain feel a little less unbearable. But the truth is, I was worn down, and I gave up on fighting the pain. My body was exhausted, my soul was tired, and the chronic fatigue was crushing. Most days, I would leave work at 2:00, crawl into bed, and sleep straight through until it was time to wake up for work the next morning—

only waking up long enough to take my medicine. That became my life.

My body was breaking down, and my spirit wasn't far behind. I knew this was more than a surgery gone wrong. And I was about to find out exactly what it was.

A SURVIVOR'S TRUTH:

Surviving pain, whether it's the loss of someone you love or of who you used to be, will break you open. In that brokenness, you will look for fast relief, expert advice, and a miracle. But here is the truth: **not every prescription is protection.** The fog of pain can make you vulnerable to anything that promises peace. Stay awake. Stay aware. What you put in your body can numb your pain, but it can also bury your power.

THE RISE BACK TAKEAWAY:

Before you swallow something, research it. Before you fill a prescription, ask why. Before you accept something, listen to your gut. You have the right to question doctors, to say no, to pause, to demand alternatives. You are not just a patient. You are the protector of your body. Stay conscious. Stay curious. Chronic pain will demand everything, but so will healing. Pick your battle, but make sure it's one you lead.

TRANSFORMATION PROMPT:

Write about one part of your life that looks fine on the outside but feels unsettled on the inside.

_____

_____

_____

_____

_____

Healing involves
discomfort, but so does
refusing to heal.
Over time, refusing to heal
is always more painful.

Chapter Nine

FOUR LETTERS, ONE CRUEL TRUTH

*F*our letters, one cruel truth: the pain wasn't going away. Diagnosis: CRPS, which stands for chronic regional pain syndrome. I referred to it as "hell." Before this, I had never heard of CRPS. I had no idea what it entailed and could find very little information available about it. The pain doctor finally gave it a name, but she didn't tell me much about it.

CRPS is a rare neurological condition that causes severe, unrelenting pain, usually in a limb after surgery or injury. This is not typical post-surgical pain. It's fire under the skin, mixed with electric shocks, and it doesn't let up. The pain is relentless.

It is believed to be caused by damage to or a malfunction of the peripheral and central nervous systems, meaning your nerves essentially go haywire. They misfire and continuously send pain signals to your brain even when there is no longer an injury.

CRPS can be triggered by something as minor as a sprain, fracture, or surgery. In my case, it was triggered by hip surgery. The condition can spread, worsen, and possibly never go away.

Common symptoms include burning, searing, and stabbing pain, allodynia (sensitivity to touch, where even light contact, like a sheet or sock, causes severe pain), hyperalgesia (increased sensitivity to pain), changes to skin color (which can turn red, blue, or exhibit a mottled appearance), swelling, temperature fluctuations, and changes in nail and hair growth. Other symptoms include stiff joints, tremors or weakness, loss of muscle control, spreading pain beyond the original injury site, emotional symptoms like anxiety and depression, social isolation due to misunderstood pain, fatigue from fighting the relentless pain, brain fog and forgetfulness, and shame for not getting better.

These symptoms highlight the complexity of CRPS, which has earned the nickname "the suicide disease" due to its ranking as one of the most painful chronic conditions known to medicine. The pain frequently exceeds that of unprepared childbirth, cancer, tooth abscess, kidney stones, and amputation without anesthesia. On the McGill Pain Index, CRPS ranks near the top, often in the 42–46 range out of a possible 50+.

It's not just physical, it's psychological torture. The constant burning and untreatable agony wear you down emotionally, mentally, and spiritually. It is isolating and exhausting, and the lack of clear answers and effective treatments exacerbates the situation. Many people feel dismissed, disbelieved, or misdiagnosed for years before anyone finally identifies the source of their suffering. The gaslighting from the medical community can be just as damaging as the pain itself.

The suicide rate for people with this condition is heartbreakingly high. Not because they are not strong, but because CRPS can strip away quality of life when it's left untreated or ignored. Chronic suffering, limited awareness, and poor treatment options can push people into hopelessness. Studies show a higher risk of suicidal thoughts among CRPS patients, and while some find remission, there is still no cure.

My foot felt like it had been dipped in fire ants and mangled in a boat motor. The pain crawled up my leg with claws, digging all the way to my knee. This wasn't surface pain. It was deep, nerve pain. Some days it felt like a vice grip crushing my foot. Other days, like nails being hammered into my toes. The burn shifted constantly from cold to hot, then full-on fire, and I couldn't escape it.

I lived in a constant state of agony with burning, swelling, throbbing. This pain was nerve-deep and soul-deep. More than once, I begged my husband to take me to the ER so they could amputate my foot. That's how brutal it was. You reach a point where you truly believe losing the limb would be better than living with that kind of pain.

Most days were just survival. I would whisper to myself, "Don't throw up. don't throw up. Just smile. Just breathe through it."

I was physically and emotionally unwell. Everything was not okay. I had reached a level of exhaustion I didn't even know existed. It wasn't just physical exhaustion—it was soul exhaustion, the kind of pain and fatigue that makes you question everything. I was so tired: tired of fighting, tired of trying, tired of explaining my pain to others who couldn't see it, tired of going to the doctors, and tired of being dismissed.

That's the part nobody sees. There was nothing visibly wrong to indicate that I was in pain. The world tends to think that if you are not limping, you must be fine, but CRPS doesn't always manifest visibly. It silently eats your soul from within.

Those suffering from CRPS may undergo treatments such as

nerve blocks, spinal cord stimulators, ketamine infusions, and physical therapy to relieve their symptoms. However, everyone experiences pain differently, making treatment essentially a trial-and-error process.

I found myself going through this trial-and-error phase as well. After my diagnosis, my pain doctor scheduled an epidural, which was more money out of my pocket. I went to the hospital and had the procedure done, but the epidural didn't even give me thirty seconds of relief. It felt like a total waste of time and money, leaving me feeling even more defeated after yet another failed attempt at pain relief.

I was pretty much in shock, going through the motions and distracting myself with deadlines and tax returns while suppressing the emotional weight of my diagnosis, something I had gotten good at over the years. But no amount of distraction could protect me from the stages of grief, and trust me, I experienced every single one.

Denial: *This can't be forever—it will go away.* I went to work as if nothing had changed, because pretending felt safer than accepting my reality.

Anger: I had so much anger toward doctors, medications, and even my own body. I kept asking myself, *How could this happen from a routine hip surgery? Why me? Why now?*

Bargaining: *If I could just rest more, push through physical therapy, or take the medications for a few more weeks...*

Depression: I experienced the kind of isolating sadness that steals your hope. I grieved the loss of my ability to move as I once had, and the thought that I might never get better terrified me. I asked myself, *Will I be able to work? What if I can't handle an eight-hour workday? What if I never get better?*

Acceptance: Not the peaceful kind, but the kind that feels like surrender, when you realize this might really be your life now. This one doesn't come easily and never really stays long. Every time I think I am at this stage, I slide right back into denial, rage, or despair. You cycle through these stages like a storm—sometimes, all in the same day.

I mourned the version of myself that could move freely, think clearly, work tirelessly, and socialize effortlessly. I lost my sense of safety in my body and the ease I had once had. I lost the version of me that could move without pain, the one who could hustle through a twelve-hour day and still meet friends for drinks after work.

The traditional stages of grief were initially intended to describe what dying individuals go through and are not necessarily applicable to survivors who experience loss or those living with chronic pain. Over time, this model has been misrepresented as a step-by-step guide for grief, implying that individuals should check off boxes and progress through each stage sequentially. In reality, it's not a staircase. It's a complex mess, like a storm. You can return to any of these stages at any time, and often, I find myself experiencing several of them within a single day, going from denial to acceptance, then back to bargaining, and finally to anger.

And here is what I have learned: emotional pain doesn't stay "emotional." It shows up in your body. Trauma, stress, and unprocessed grief have a way of bubbling to the surface until you feel them physically. That's exactly what was happening to me.

What I was experiencing wasn't just a malfunction of my nerves. It was grief and loss that my body could no longer hold inside. My hip pain was only the entry point. All the grief I had buried, all the trauma I had numbed, had nowhere left to go, so my body carried it for me.

Every unshed tear, every scream I swallowed, settled into my muscles and nerves until my emotional pain became physical pain. It turned into my constant companion, more reliable than any friend. It was as if my anguish had taken on a body of its own, radiating from my feet to my chest, a constant reminder of everything I had lost.

Here's the thing: It's not just in your head. Science backs this up. When trauma, grief, or stress go unprocessed, the nervous system stays stuck on high alert. Cortisol and adrenaline flood your body. Rest and repair never come. Muscles stay tense, inflammation rises, and pain signals misfire. It is not just emotional burnout—it's biological chaos.

Dr. Bessel van der Kolk says it best: "The body keeps the score." He is a world-renowned psychiatrist who has spent decades studying trauma and its impact on both the mind and body. His book, *The Body Keeps the Score*, has become one of the most influential works on trauma recovery. In it, Dr. van der Kolk explains how unhealed pain doesn't just live in our memories, but in our nervous systems, our sleep, even our health. My body kept track of every score, every unspoken word, every year spent pretending that I was fine. My nervous system remembered what I always tried to forget.

I wasn't weak or being dramatic. I was carrying pain that my body was never meant to endure. When you numb your feelings for too long, your body screams even while your mouth stays silent. Emotional pain doesn't disappear when you suppress it. It relocates to your joints, nerves, gut, and sleep. I learned that healing is not just emotional, but also cellular. You don't just feel it—you become it.

One divine detour in all of this is that I quit drinking. It was more of an accidental sobriety, but I took it. In all the chaos of pain, something shifted in me. I could finally see what was silencing me, what was draining me, and what I could no longer carry.

A SURVIVOR'S TRUTH:

Some pain doesn't pass. Some healing doesn't mean returning to what you were.

CRPS didn't just change how I moved—it changed how I saw everything.

And the truth? You can't medicate your way back to who you were before trauma, but you can rebuild from where you are, piece by brutal piece.

Your nervous system remembers everything, so teach it how to feel safe again—slowly and on your terms. You don't have to be cured to be powerful.

THE RISE BACK TAKEAWAY:

Your body is not broken. It's begging to be heard.

CRPS taught me to stop waging war on my pain and start listening to it.

When you treat your symptoms like enemies, you miss the message.

Pain is information, not identity.

Create a "Pain Journal"—track what makes the pain worse,

what brings calm, and how your nervous system responds to different environments.

Test one holistic ritual: breathwork, contrast therapy, gentle stretching, or walking.

Honor your body's limits without apologizing for them.

There is no honor in pushing yourself to exhaustion.

Radical healing begins when you stop performing strength and start practicing surrender.

TRANSFORMATION PROMPT:

Where are you pretending to be strong, and what might shift if you let yourself lay it down?

_____

_____

_____

_____

_____

The strongest souls are

not born from ease.

They are built in the dark,

brick by brutal brick,

when no one is watching.

Chapter Ten

SOUL WAKE-UP

I didn't hit a classic rock bottom. Early on in my trauma, I learned how to suppress my needs and keep emotions locked down because falling apart never felt safe. I became the "don't worry about me, I am fine" kind of girl. But eventually, I realized drinking had trapped me in a life that was too small for me. Playing small wasn't noble—it dimmed my light and made me disappear in my own life.

After my surgery, though, everything changed. I was so sick and broken that drinking didn't even sound good anymore. My body was wrecked. My soul was tired. Vodka, which once felt like relief, now felt like poison. I couldn't keep using alcohol to escape grief, shame, or the chronic pain that had taken over my life. This wasn't anyone else's definition of rock bottom — but it was mine.

The pain was constant and consumed my every thought. I had to start asking myself some hard questions: Who am I when I am not escaping? Who am I when I finally sit still in the truth of my pain? My CRPS diagnosis forced me to rely heavily on my husband. I couldn't go to the grocery store. I couldn't drive very far. Pressing my foot on the accelerator for too long sent shocks of nerve pain through me.

On top of that, my glute and quad on the surgery side still wouldn't engage. Three times a week, I went to the chiropractor to get things firing again, only for them to shut down again. When this happened, the muscle would press on a nerve and cause a whole different kind of nerve pain. After my appointments, I would cry all the way back to work, then sit down to do tax returns as if nothing was wrong. My boss had a hip replacement just months after mine and was thriving in recovery, while I was still a complete mess. Every day, I walked into the office saying, "Something is wrong. Very wrong."

Five months post-op, my hormones completely flatlined, likely from the steroid injections, the stress, and the trauma stacked on trauma. Even though I had already been through menopause, suddenly I was back to hot flashes, night sweats, and relentless inflammation.

Finally, I turned to another holistic practitioner in my town. She studied my blood work and helped me find supplements that actually supported my body. I shifted to an anti-inflammatory diet, began eating with intention, and started using a hormone cream that lowered my blood pressure and calmed the fire in my hip and sciatica. It wasn't perfect, but slowly, my body began to respond. Slowly, I began to believe healing was possible.

During this time, I went back to my general practitioner for more blood work and a fresh perspective. Instead, she tried to put me on two new prescriptions: Cymbalta and ropinirole. She was convinced they would "fix my mood" and bring back my "pre-pain personality."

She asked if I had restless legs, and I told her no, but she wouldn't let it go. She kept circling back, rephrasing the question, almost trying to convince me I had Restless Legs Syndrome so she could prescribe ropinirole. It didn't matter how many times I said no, she insisted it would help with my pain. Sitting there, I felt like my words didn't matter, like I was being shoved into a box that didn't fit. I didn't need a new label—I needed answers.

I declined both of the prescriptions and left the office defeated. Out of frustration, I googled the medications. What I found was alarming.

Ropinirole (brand name Requip) is used for Parkinson's and Restless Legs Syndrome. It's a dopamine agonist, which basically means it tricks your brain into thinking it has more dopamine—the chemical tied to movement, mood, and motivation. The side effects read like a nightmare: sudden sleep attacks (even while driving), hallucinations, impulse-control problems like gambling or binge eating.

And then there was Cymbalta. It's an antidepressant, an SNRI that raises serotonin and norepinephrine levels to help with mood and pain. On paper, it sounds helpful. But buried in the warnings were the very words that stopped me cold: may cause suicidal thoughts or behavior. Other risks included liver damage (especially with alcohol use), severe withdrawal symptoms, and something called "serotonin syndrome," which can cause hallucinations and muscle stiffness.

That was my breaking point. At that moment, I realized no one was coming to save me. I realized I had to take control of my health. I couldn't blindly follow prescriptions that didn't even match my symptoms.

I was in unimaginable pain, and the medical answer was

medication that made me want to disappear. How backward is that? How broken is a system that offers a drug that deepens the darkness I was already fighting to survive? I was being chemically shoved toward the edge while begging for a way out.

I had to become my own advocate, protector, and gatekeeper. After surviving excruciating pain and absolute hell, I wasn't about to be reduced to another prescription with a warning label for suicidal thoughts or impulse control. I was done outsourcing my healing to a system that never actually listened.

Every doctor I saw just wanted to slap a prescription on my pain, hoping it would silence my complaints. I explained to all of them that my family has a history of suicide. Not one single doctor listened to me. Eventually, I began asking harder questions.

Let me be clear: I am not against medication. There are people whose lives depend on it. This is not about shame, either—it's about awareness. *This is my story, my body, my breaking point.* Just remember that you are allowed to ask questions. Trust your instincts, do your research, and say no when something doesn't feel right.

Right now, the only thing that works for me is tramadol, just enough to take the edge off so I can sleep. Do I worry about dependency? Every single day. I know these medications lose their punch, and then your body wants more. I have watched that story play out before, and it terrifies me.

So I take it carefully, intentionally, and with eyes wide open. I don't pretend to have all the answers. I am simply doing the best I can with the hand I have been dealt, making choices from clarity, not desperation. Pain makes it so easy to panic, to grab for whatever promises relief. But I have lived long enough (and lost enough) to know that desperation comes with a cost.

I know this medication will not work forever, but I hold on to the hope that by the time that day comes, I will have found a doctor who truly listens and sees me as more than a chart. Until then, I will keep showing up for myself, one clear conscious choice at a time.

That's what rising looks like when the pain doesn't leave. It's steady, intentional, and soul-led. I no longer silence my instincts to make someone else feel like the expert. I have lived in this body every single day of my life, and no one knows it better than I do. While I am committed to healing, I also refuse to suffer just to prove a point. There is no honor in living in pain 24/7. The real work is learning how to find enough relief to make it through the days without slipping into dependence or fear. It's not black and white. It's a gray in-between where grace and grit have to coexist.

So, I started researching and journaling. I tracked what made the pain worse and what made it bearable. I stopped waiting for someone else to fix me, and I swear my body whispered, *Thank you for finally listening*. That's when I started to participate in my healing with real intention.

I realized I had two choices: sit on the couch moaning from the pain, or start moving. So I walked. One block at a time. My husband came with me because sometimes my legs would give out without warning. I started with a single block, and by the end of that block, I was exhausted. I bought new tennis shoes, still a size too big and too wide. My husband joked that I looked like a toddler learning how to walk, and he wasn't wrong. That one block was all I could manage at that time. For someone who used to crush CrossFit workouts, measuring progress by a single block was humbling. But I kept going.

After a week, I worked up to a thousand steps. My hip would

throb, and every nerve in my foot would light up like fire when I stopped, but I did it. Oddly enough, my feet tolerated the walk itself—it was afterward that hell set in.

That was my starting line. The beginning of my comeback. I walked when I could, rested when I had to. Sometimes, the pain knocked me out for fifteen hours straight. And I had to retrain my brain not to panic at the slightest touch to my foot. Desensitization became part of my daily routine—small steps toward wearing shoes again without every nerve screaming.

Desensitization is a process of gently retraining your nervous system to respond better to sensory input. It's slow, repetitive, and uncomfortable, but it's powerful when done consistently. It became a daily ritual of rubbing (introducing different textures to the affected area, such as a soft washcloth, cotton ball, or Velcro), tapping (light tapping in a rhythmic pattern using your fingertips or soft tool), breathing (inhaling through the nose, exhaling through the mouth), and repeating. I was teaching my nervous system that I was safe now.

Around that time, I started reading *The Mind-Body Prescription* by Dr. John E. Sarno, a book that completely changed how I viewed healing. It was written decades ago, but it hit me like lightning. It taught me that chronic pain is not purely physical. It's also emotional, neurological, and cellular. I started realizing that my body was screaming truths that I had never made space to hear.

Then I discovered another book: *Joy Through the Journey* by Amberly Lago. In it, she teaches about gratitude, and she also lives with CRPS, so right away, I felt seen. She shares tools for gratitude, mindfulness, and mindset shifts that helped her move from merely surviving to truly thriving, even amid physical and emotional chaos. She taught me that even when your body is betraying you, you can still take back your power.

Her book changed my life. It emphasizes gratitude, and it taught me to identify three small joys each morning, a practice I began on my walks and continue to this day: a cool breeze, a kind smile, and the fact that I woke up. This practice became my ritual, especially on the days I felt anything but grateful.

I also started a gratitude checklist at work during tax season. My boss and I would write down daily what we were grateful for. Mine were typically the little things: *"I didn't spill my coffee," "My favorite pen still has ink in it."* I am not kidding when I say small, but those small wins became my anchors. Applying gratitude to my life shifted my perspective. For a brief moment, I didn't feel so broken. I began to believe that maybe I could survive this and that I wasn't alone.

I joined a Facebook group for people with CRPS, hoping to connect with others, but their posts were full of despair. That Facebook page handed out pain stories like communion wafers in church. I couldn't absorb their grief and carry mine, too, so I realized I had to leave that group. Protecting my peace is such a major part of my healing.

In April, after tax season ended, I saw that Amberly Lago was hosting an event, and I felt deep in my gut that I needed to go, even if I didn't feel ready. Honestly, I signed up before I felt ready because I knew that if I waited until I felt good enough, I would never go. This event was my first big outing since my surgery, my first flight, my first hotel stay, and the first time I ventured beyond the safety of my home.

My last outing had been right before my surgery. I took a quick trip to Cancun for a retreat with some amazing ladies. That trip took an unexpected turn when I got caught in Hurricane Helene. I had never been in a hurricane before, and it was terrifying. I ended up stuck in my hotel room and had to stay an extra day because all flights were grounded due to the strong winds and rain. I returned home just in time for my surgery the following week. I miss being able to go somewhere on a whim, to slip into adventure without thinking twice. More than that, I miss life as I knew it.

At Amberly's event, I was still experiencing a lot of pain. I felt overstimulated, anxious, and unsure if my body could handle the experience, but something inside me knew I had to try. Being in that room was everything I didn't know I needed. Surrounded by people chasing something greater, I listened to speakers share their truths with raw honesty and unshakable strength. To sit in a room full of fire and not feel alone in mine was powerful.

That weekend, I learned that I am not my diagnosis. My past doesn't define me, and there is no way I am done yet. I still have chapters to write, battles to fight, and a life to live that refuses to be cut short by pain. I felt hope, real and steady hope, which I had not felt in a long time.

While in Dallas for the event, I scheduled an appointment with a neurosurgeon who was highly recommended, since I still needed answers. I had already gotten an MRI before I went because some doctors still insisted that my back was to blame for this pain. After reviewing the MRI, the neurosurgeon told me that it was one thousand percent *not* my back, that it was CRPS.

This confirmed what I already knew, but I needed to hear it again. He mentioned that a spinal cord stimulator might be the only real option for pain relief, but he warned that even that might not help. I told him, "I can't take pills anymore. My brain just can't handle them." He completely understood and wished me well, along with a couple of "I am so sorrys."

I left his office with clarity, but not because I was ready to say yes to the spinal cord stimulator. I had done the research, read the studies, and watched the testimonials. For me, the risks far outweighed the relief. It was invasive surgery with no guarantee that it would work. The possibility of more nerve damage, infection, or trading one kind of pain for another wasn't a gamble I was willing to take. I am not saying it's wrong for everyone, but I have learned to trust my gut. What I needed was sustainable relief, not another trauma wrapped in hope.

That weekend, something in me shifted, and my perspective changed. It didn't erase the pain or undo all my losses, but it changed the way I carried them.

I used to wake up every day furious at the fire in my foot. I hated feeling like a distant version of the woman I used to be. Even now, I struggle with the fact that walking is all I can do, because it never feels like enough. I miss my CrossFit days, being strong and gritty, fueled by sweat, chalk, and the clang of a barbell hitting the floor. That version of me was relentless, focused, and disciplined. And I want her back.

I started asking myself, *What if this pain is my teacher? What if the last eighteen years of loss were preparing me to live deeper, not smaller? What if all the things, like busyness, control, CrossFit, the drinking, the doing, were actually distractions that were keeping me from the real work? The soul work. The kind that strips you down and makes you ask: Who are you without the noise?*

I had to change everything. I had to stop shrinking myself to fit in a life that no longer existed.

Now, instead of lifting heavy weights, I celebrate each step I take. Walking doesn't make me weak—it makes me a different kind of strong. Some days, resilience looks like movement, and other days, it looks like rest. Now I find strength in the silence, in the small act of walking and choosing to keep going. Even when everything hurts, at least I can walk.

I had to make peace with this new version of myself. I can only do what my body allows me to do, and that has to be enough. Now, I often walk up to five miles a day. Those walks have become sacred to me. I call them my "soul journey walks."

It's not about weight loss, step counts, or tracking progress anymore. It's about being present. It's about choosing movement when everything in my past has urged me to stay stuck.

I walk under the sun, letting it warm my skin and remind me that I am alive. I breathe in the fresh air like it's medicine. I listen to podcasts that nourish my mind. "Garbage in, garbage out," I always say.

Sometimes, my husband or daughter joins me, and we walk and talk without distractions or pretending, just real, meaningful, soul-deep conversations. I never made time for those conversations when I was merely surviving, but now I crave them.

Those walks saved me. They have become my therapy, my nervous system reset, my sacred ritual, and my proof that I am still healing, even if it hurts.

Strength looks totally different to me now. Strength is rising from the ashes. It's rebuilding my life from ground zero. It's saying no to the easy escape. It's healing, even when it hurts. That's the kind of strength I carry now because there was a time when I didn't even recognize myself in the mirror.

My husband and I talk about this often: the real possibility that if I had said yes to every prescription pushed across the desk at me... oxycodone, hydrocodone, Cymbalta, Requip, Lyrica, gabapentin. My story could have looked very different. I could have ended up addicted, numbed out, suicidal, maybe even dead. That thought chills me. The only reason I didn't go down that road is because my gut screamed no... and because I had already lived the nightmare of watching my mom's life unravel under the weight of pills.

There's no denying it—God has shown up in every corner of my story. Not in big, dramatic ways, but in the quiet nudges that pulled me back to life when I wanted to give up. Faith isn't just a Sunday thing. It's the steady breath that gets me through hard days and the reason I keep putting one foot in front of the other when I want to stop.

I've learned that healing can't be done alone. You need people (*your* people) who know what it means to break and rebuild. That's why community matters. That's why the suicide LOSS Team changed everything for me. It showed me the power of walking beside others who have been through the fire and still choose to rise. Healing requires honesty, and honesty needs safety. Find your tribe, and keep them close.

Years ago, I got a tattoo that says, *"The sweet is never as sweet without the sour."* Back then, I thought it just meant I appreciated joy more because I had tasted pain. Now, I feel it in my bones. Peace doesn't land the same if you have never lived through chaos. Purpose doesn't shine the same if you have never been lost. I used to love the quote, "Not all who wander are lost." But here is the cold, hard truth... I had to get lost to finally find myself.

The sweet (peace, purpose, healing) only hits this deep because I have tasted the sour. The suffering showed me what I am made of. And now, the sweet is not just sweet—it's sacred, because I fought like hell for it.

I may not lift the way I used to, drink like I used to, or numb like I used to, but I fight harder now. With every step I take toward truth and wholeness, I fight with clarity and conviction.

Now it's your turn. You can rise, you can rebuild. It won't be easy, but I promise you this: it will be worth it. The life that broke you open... might just be the one that sets you free.

A SURVIVOR'S TRUTH:

Emotional pain doesn't disappear. It just relocates.
To your joints, your nerves, your gut, your sleep until you feel it. I promise that it will find ways to be felt. The body won't lie, even when you do. Listen to it. Healing doesn't begin when the pain ends. Healing begins when you decide to face it, one raw step at a time.

THE RISE BACK TAKEAWAY

Your body is speaking. Your spirit is speaking. Stop tuning them out, and start paying attention. Write it down. Test what helps, let go of what hurts, and keep what makes you stronger.
You don't need to overhaul your entire life overnight.
Choose one small shift: A walk, a journal entry, a conversation, a prayer, and stick with it. Tiny choices stacked together create big wins.

TRANSFORMATION PROMPT:

What story are you ready to stop telling, and what new story are you brave enough to begin?

_____

_____

_____

_____

_____

If you don't know what to chase next, chase yourself. Chase healing. Chase peace. Chase becoming the healthiest, happiest, most healed, most present, most confident version of yourself. When you rise, the path will, too.

Chapter Eleven

THE RISE BACK

his chapter is not a clean ending. It's the moment I finally looked in the mirror and saw her again... the woman I abandoned for so long. For years, I survived by smiling through it, staying strong, and holding it all in. But the truth is, I was numb and disconnected, just going through the motions.

Survival got me here, but it wasn't enough anymore. I realized I had a choice: stay stuck in the shell of myself or become the woman I was meant to be. My story was never about having everything figured out—it was about falling apart again and again and still choosing to rise.

For eighteen years, I drowned my emotions with silence and alcohol, thinking it made me stronger. I showed up, but I wasn't living. I was only performing. Now I am obsessed with healing. Maybe it's not an obsession—maybe it's an awakening. I am starting to remember that being human means I get to evolve. These days, when I look in the mirror, I don't see a stranger anymore. I see the woman who lived, who fought, who stumbled, who got back up. The one I left behind. The one I get to honor now.

I have so much compassion for the girl I used to be. I don't shame her anymore. She did the best she could with what she had. She was drowning in silence and carrying pain she didn't know how to name.

Here is what I have learned: you can't create a new reality with an old mentality. I clung to my old ways like they were life rafts—hustling, drinking, numbing, surviving. They felt safe because they were familiar. But healing demanded more. It demanded honesty. It demanded that I get uncomfortable. It demanded I stop giving away my power and finally do the healing work.

And so I do. Every single day.

Every version of me was necessary—the wife, the mother, the daughter, the friend, the sister, the drinker, the partier, the wild one, the one who never asked for help but needed it more than anyone else. I don't erase them; I honor them because they didn't ruin me.

They raised me.

Throughout this last part of my journey, I have weaned myself off every prescription, except tramadol. Trazodone was the last to go and the one that had been with me the longest. I quit taking two blood pressure pills after starting a hormone cream that made my blood pressure come down. Turns out, your body will fight for you when you stop fighting against it.

Once I began paying attention to how I fueled my body, I realized I didn't need the heartburn meds either. I even came off cholesterol meds cold turkey, always wondering if they played a part in my nerve pain.

But getting off trazodone has been the hardest. I have weaned off slowly, but the insomnia and brain fog are no joke. Eighteen years of relying on it unraveled piece by piece, and I am still feeling it. But I want clarity more than comfort, and I knew I couldn't stay on it forever.

Let me be clear: I am not anti-medication. If you need it, please take it. Medication saves lives. This is just my journey, and I worked closely with doctors through every step. I didn't wake up and ditch my pills—I got curious. I listened to my body, asked better questions, and made choices that matched where I was in my healing process.

But physical healing was only one part of it.

The emotional weight of suicide loss cuts deep. There is nothing simple about navigating that kind of pain, and we have to break the silence surrounding it. Shame thrives in silence. If you have been carrying the weight of what-ifs, hear me: it wasn't your fault. Honor your loved one not by drowning in guilt, but by speaking the truth, ending the stigma, and holding space for yourself and for others surviving the unimaginable.

Community saved me. I found people who understood suicide loss. They didn't fix it. They just got it, and that was everything. Slowly, the fog lifted. I discovered healthier ways to cope, and I connected with women who were rising from their own ashes. They were honest, authentic, and committed to healing. Their courage helped awaken mine.

Surrender is the starting point for true healing. Surrender is not weakness. It's not giving up, and it's not quitting. Surrender is letting go of what no longer serves you. It's loosening your grip on pain, perfectionism, and old plans that keep you stuck.

But here is the question that I still wrestled with: how do I hold space for both pain and peace? How do I keep choosing to heal when the grief still lingers?

For me, the answer is journaling.

I used to think journaling was pointless. Seriously, I thought it was for teenage girls with glitter pens. I didn't understand that journaling is not about performance—it's about processing. When you have carried pain in your body, your silence, and your mind, it needs somewhere to go. If you don't let it out, it will leak out as anxiety, anger, exhaustion, addiction, or emotional shutdown.

Journaling became my place without judgment or shame. A place to tell the truth I couldn't say out loud yet. A place where buried thoughts surfaced and where I began to rescue myself.

Here is what worked for me:

Start with the same three prompts every day:

What am I feeling right now?

What am I avoiding?

What do I need today?

Keep it messy. Forget punctuation, spelling, or making sense. Set a five-minute timer—you will be shocked by what comes out.

End with gratitude. Every morning, I write down three things I am grateful for. I learned this from Amberly Lago, and it anchors me on the heaviest days. Gratitude doesn't erase the hard, but it makes sure the hard doesn't drown out the good.

Here is the hard truth: everyone wants growth, but not everyone will embrace the discomfort that comes with it. For years, I didn't. I numbed instead. I hated how I felt, but I stayed in the loop of survival because it felt safer than change.

Discomfort is part of growth. When it shows up, your brain will flood you with excuses... "It's not the right time," "I need more clarity," "I am fine where I am." Those are not truths—they are trauma responses. Comfort feels safe, but it will keep you stuck in a life you have already outgrown.

So the real question is: are you willing to trade comfort for growth? Not forever, but just long enough to prove to yourself that you are stronger than your survival patterns.

Start small. Pick one thing that stretches you. One thing that forces you to show up even when it's uncomfortable. You need a dragon to slay. Mine was writing this book.

Commit to it for six months. One habit, one truth, one promise to yourself. Maybe it's cutting out alcohol. Maybe it's journaling daily. Maybe it's lifting heavy, walking outside, meditating, or finally sharing your story.

That last one, sharing your story. It is one of the bravest things you can do. Speaking your truth doesn't just set it free.

It sets *you* free.

As I close this chapter, I want to tell you something I wish someone had told me years ago: I think you are brave. Not because you have it all figured out, but because you're still here. Still breathing. Still willing to rise.

For years, I thought bravery meant conquering mountains or holding it all together. But bravery looks a lot more like surviving the unthinkable and daring to keep going anyway. If only we could see ourselves as brave instead of broken, how different the road might feel.

Bravery doesn't erase the pain, but it reframes it. It gives you permission to keep moving forward, even with the weight you carry. When you call yourself brave, you stop waiting for rescue. You realize you have already been rescuing yourself all along.

Your mind can either anchor you in survival or launch you toward purpose. Storms are inevitable. You don't get to choose that. But you do get to choose how you navigate them. You can drift, you can drown, or you can rise. You already know my choice.

You are not here to disappear into silence.
You are here to rise—unapologetically.
This is not the end. This is your Rise Back.
I know how hard it is to rise when everything inside you wants to collapse, so I want to hand you some practices that helped me rise when I thought I couldn't.
This is what pulled me out of survival again and again.
This is what became my lifeline.

THE R.I.S.E. U.P. METHOD™

A Framework for Taking Back Your Power

R – Reach Out Before You Shut Down
Isolation feels safe, but it's dangerous.
Pain thrives in silence, and shame grows in the dark.
Whether it's a trusted friend, a coach, a therapist, or a support group—reach out. Connection is your lifeline.

I – Ink It Out
Your thoughts need a place to go that is not your body.
Journaling helped me process grief, anger, confusion, and clarity.
You don't need perfection, you need honesty.

S – Sit with It

Stop running from discomfort.

Grief demands to be felt.

Sit with the anger. Sit with the fear. Sit with the ache.

It's not there to break you, it's there to move you.

E – Embrace Who You Are Becoming

You don't owe anyone your old self.

You are allowed to evolve. You are allowed to grow.

The version of you that's rising is wiser, stronger, and closer to who you were always meant to be.

U – Unlearn the Lies

Grief tells us stories that are not true: You are too broken.

You should be over it. You did something wrong.

It's time to unlearn all of it. Replace shame with truth.

Take back your voice.

P – Protect Your Peace

This is sacred work.

Not everyone deserves access to your healing. Protect your energy. Guard your nervous system.

You don't have to explain your boundaries to people who only want access, not understanding.

Here is what this looked like in my own healing:

I got radically honest with myself. No more pretending. No more numbing. I started asking hard questions: What am I pretending not to feel? What is this pain trying to teach me?

I cleaned up my inputs. What I consumed—mentally, emotionally, physically—mattered. Garbage in, garbage out. I started treating food as fuel and filtered what voices I let shape me.

I embraced the silence. Quitting drinking was lonely. The silence was deafening. But stillness gave me clarity. I started to hear myself again.

I grieved out loud. Suicide loss carries stigma. People go silent, and that silence feels like a second loss. I learned that speaking my truth not only freed me but gave others permission to speak theirs.

I found community. Healing doesn't happen in isolation. I found people who didn't need my explanations. They just let me be. Sometimes, you need to borrow someone else's courage until you find your own.

I practiced self-compassion daily. I don't criticize the old me anymore. I thank her. She survived what could have destroyed her. She kept showing up. Every version of me was doing the best she could—and every one of them was necessary.

Don't wait to be saved. Don't wait for the storm to pass. Don't wait for perfect clarity.

Rise anyway. Burn anyway. Heal anyway.

This is not the end.

This is your Rise Back.

A SURVIVOR'S TRUTH:

You don't need to hit rock bottom to rise. You just need to decide that surviving is no longer enough. The healing you crave will not come in a bottle or a quick fix. It lives in your choices, your courage, and your willingness to keep going when it hurts. You are not broken. You are waking up. You don't rise because it's easy. You rise because staying in the dark starts to hurt more than climbing out. Healing doesn't come wrapped in clarity or perfection—it comes through surrender, truth-telling, and choosing to live when you have every reason to shut down.

THE RISE BACK TAKEAWAY:

You want healing? Then stop playing small with your pain.
Stop waiting for the perfect timing, the perfect plan, the perfect you.
Pick the hard thing.
Do it relentlessly.
Disrupt every lie that told you this is where it ends.
Because it doesn't end here.
Not in the darkness. Not in the silence. Not in the shame.
You are not here to be buried.
You are here to rise—soul first, fists clenched, heart wide open.
Burn it down if you have to.
Rebuild with truth.
And don't just rise.
Rise savage.

TRANSFORMATION PROMPT:

What does your soul need to feel whole again, and what are you
finally willing to do about it?

_____

_____

_____

_____

_____

I am the rise back.
Not the collapse, but the rise
that came after.
I stopped waiting to be
rescued. I stopped apologizing
for my story. I faced the
wreckage, stood in the fire,
and rebuilt something fierce
from everything that
tried to bury me.

AFTERWORD

I AM THE RISE BACK.

Not the collapse, but the rise that came after.

I stopped waiting to be rescued and stopped apologizing for my story.

I faced the wreckage, stood in the fire, and rebuilt something fierce from everything that tried to bury me.

I didn't just survive this time—I led myself home.

If you are still here, it means you didn't look away.

You walked through the wreckage with me of grief, heartbreak, alcohol, chronic pain, and every soul-crushing moment in between.

You have seen what it looks like to survive experiences that no one ever signs up for. More importantly, you have witnessed what it truly means to rise. This book is not just my story. It's a mirror, a reminder that no matter how broken you feel, you are not beyond repair.

You will not wake up one day and be magically healed.

Instead, one breath, one choice, one brutally honest moment at a time, you will feel yourself coming back to life, not as who you were before, but as someone deeper, wiser, and more awake.

Thank you. Thank you for showing up for yourself, for your pain, and for your potential. Thank you for holding space for this truth. I hope my story stirred something awake in you, something fierce, something that refuses to stay silent.

I don't want you to close this book and go back to playing small. Let this be your Rise Back. You have what it takes to rebuild your life with soul, grit, and savage self-compassion.

You are not meant to just survive—you are meant to rise.

Want to keep rising together?

I will be launching a coaching course soon to walk with survivors as they rebuild their souls and rise after suicide loss. Follow me on Instagram for more details.

This is not just a book. It's a movement, and I want you in it.

Let's stay connected:

Email: tiff@risesavage.com

Instagram: @ tiffaneychilders

Website: www.risesavage.com

Feel free to send me a message, share your breakthroughs, or ask me anything.

We heal in community. We rise together.

I would be honored to walk alongside you as you write your next chapter. This is your invitation to rise, not in spite of the pain, but because of it. This is The Rise Back to who you truly are. You are not broken. You are beautiful. Let's burn the silence together.

ACKNOWLEDGMENTS

This book wouldn't exist without the people who held me together while I was falling apart and stood by me while I rebuilt my Rise Back.

To my husband—my person, my anchor—we have lived half of our lives side by side, and you have stood with me through every storm, every silence, every chapter of this journey. Your unwavering love has been my safe place.

To Stratton and Mia, you are my greatest reasons to keep going —my heartbeats. You saved me, and you didn't even know it. Being your mom gave me purpose when I couldn't find my own. You are, without question, the greatest accomplishments of my life.

To my sister—my soul twin, my constant—we survived the unimaginable together. You have held my hand through every wild, gut-wrenching, beautiful chapter of this life. You are my heart in human form.

To Fuss, my ride-or-die, you rode your motorcycle to my dad's house all those years ago—first on the scene, and you never left. Your loyalty and love have carried me through some of my roughest times.

To my mother-in-law, who has loved me like her own from the very beginning. Your quiet, steady love has been one of the greatest gifts of my life.

To my stepdad, thank you for staying when you didn't have to. You never walked away, and I will never stop being grateful that you stayed.

To Amberly Lago, you are more than a friend. You are the sister I didn't grow up with, but somehow found along the way. Thank you for walking this road with me, for believing in me, and for showing me what resilience looks like in action.

And to Myrna Hill, my boss, friend, and patient witness to all my chaos, thank you for showing up with grace, even when I showed up with pain, for understanding the days I couldn't explain, and for giving me space to heal while still believing in my strength.

And finally, to every survivor reading this—you are the reason these words exist. This book is for you. Your courage reminds me that silence can be shattered, shame can be dismantled, and life after loss is possible. You are braver than you know.

Thank you all for loving me through the dark chapters. Your belief in me is part of why I found my way to The Rise Back.

THANK YOU FOR READING MY BOOK!

Thank you for walking through these pages with me.
I would love to give you a free bonus gift as my way
of saying thanks, no strings attached!

Scan the QR Code:

*I appreciate your interest in my book and value your feedback, as it helps
me improve future versions. I would appreciate it if you could leave your
invaluable review on Amazon.com with your feedback. Thank you!*